THE SNOOK BOOK

A Complete Angler's Guide

by

Frank Sargeant

Book I in the Inshore Library

by Larsen's Outdoor Publishing

ISBN 0-936513-13-6

Library of Congress 90-063532

Published by:

LARSEN'S OUTDOOR PUBLISHING
2640 Elizabeth Place
Lakeland, FL 33813

PRINTED IN THE UNITED STATES OF AMERICA

9 10

ACKNOWLEDGEMENTS

My sincere thanks to the many fishermen, guides, biologists and marine scientists who have contributed to the production of this book. Among those who deserve special mention are guide Scott Moore, who has probably caught more snook than any man alive, and probably taught more anglers to enjoy the snook arts than any other guide. Also very helpful was Larry Mendez of Shoalwater Boats, who frequently made me a guest in his backcountry adventures. Guides Paul Hawkins and Russ Sirmons also shared snook secrets with me, as did David Fairbanks of MirrOlure and Steve Marusak of Cotee Jigs. Roy Williams, now assistant director of the Marine Fisheries Commission, was frequently helpful in my fisheries education, as were snook experts Jerry Bruger, Ron Taylor, Jim Whittington and Danny Roberts of the Florida Department of Natural Resources. Ed Irby, formerly the east coast snook researcher and now a Tallahassee exec for DNR, was also instructive.

COVER: illustration of a leaping snook is by St. Petersburg artist and snook guide Russ Sirmons. Sirmons sculpts his exquisite works in glass with sandblasting equipment and hours of dedication. He accepts commissions to do fish and birds of all species. He can be reached at (813) 526-2090.

PREFACE

Snook fishing is a growing sport, because snook numbers have increased steadily in recent years, and also because more and more anglers are discovering the joys in inshore saltwater fishing. This book is dedicated to those growing legions of snook fishermen, both experts and those who would like to become experts. It's based on more than 20 years of fishing with the finest snook anglers in Florida and Central America. All the basics are covered to get the novice started, but there's also extensive, in-depth material that should make any snooker a better fisherman. Every angler has his own unique tricks and stores of know-how, and the author has tried to include the best from the many fine fishermen who have allowed him to share their boats.

The coverage is year-around, and applies to snook where ever they are found, from the glassy shallows of the West Coast to the rolling green inlets of the Atlantic shore, as well as throughout the wild, dingy waters of the Everglades, Mexico, Costa Rica and points south.

The Snook Book is also a compendium of the best in snook tackle, boats and the other piles of gear dear to a fisherman's heart. And those interested in the biology, habitat and habits of *Centropomis undecimalis*--and his related cousins--will also find much to ponder here.

Finally, you'll find this is a book that names names--there's a listing of Florida's top guides, along with their telephone numbers. A book can take you only so far--if you want to jump to the ranks of experts in a single day, the guide can do the job.

CONTENTS

ABOUT THE AUTHOR

Frank Sargeant is outdoors editor of the Tampa Tribune, and a senior writer for Southern Outdoors, Southern Saltwater and BassMaster magazines. He was formerly an editor for CBS Publications Division, and a writer for Disney World Publications, as well as southern editor for Outdoor Life. His writing and photos have appeared in a wide variety of publications, including Field & Stream, Sports Afield, Popular Mechanics, Popular Science and the Reader's Digest. He was a fishing guide before becoming a writer and editor. He holds a masters degree in English and Creative Writing from Ohio University, and has taught writing at the high school and college level. He has fished for snook throughout Florida and Central America for more than 20 years. He lives on the Little Manatee River, one of Florida's best snook waters.

CHAPTER 1

INTRODUCTION:
WELCOME TO SNOOK COUNTRY

THERE'S NOTHING COMMON about the common snook, *Centropomis undecimalis*. The snook is a backstreet-fighter, without match. The linesider hits harder than any other inshore gamefish, pulls like a bonito and jumps like a tarpon. And it does it all in tangled little mangrove creeks too narrow for an alligator to turn around.

Hooking a big snook in such water is like dropping a grenade into a garbage can, then hopping inside and pulling on the lid.

Beyond the excitement of the battles, the snook is found in some of the most ecologically beautiful country our nation has to offer. Snook are subtropical fish. That means that, like orange trees, mangroves and manatees, they are limited to areas that stay warm year around. Water temperature below 70 degrees F is tough on snook, and water temperatures below 60 kill them. That means they're limited primarily to Florida, within the United States, and not all of Florida, at that.

The "snook line" runs roughly from Port Richey, on the west coast, to Cape Canaveral, on the east coast. There are pockets further north, on both sides--the spring-fed rivers at Homosassa and Crystal River, for example--but for dependable action, snook anglers cast their eyes (and their lures) toward the southern half of the peninsula. A few years of unusually warm weather can temporarily move the snook line further north, and in recent seasons there have been many snook caught in the Daytona Beach area. But the

11

Centropomis undecimalis, the common snook, is also known as the linesider, the robalo, and coincidentally, the "sargeant fish". It's a subtropical species, found only in the southern half of the Florida peninsula and southward through the Tropics.

Christmas freeze of 1989 killed most of these splinter populations. The consistent production areas are all further south.

Prime snook country is an angler's dream, estuary waters where the fresh water flowing from the coastal marshes and rivers mixes with the salt of the seas. Snook country can be mangrove country, laced with the labyrinthian winding of blackwater creeks that run into the land for miles, necking down so narrow they're barely wide enough to allow passage of a water moccasin. Snook country can be the inshore grass flats, clear, warm shallows where turtle grass and manatee grass spread in a gray-green carpet filled with marine life. Snook country can be a deep coastal pass, where the green waters foam and boil with the strong flows of spring. It can be the last oyster bar at the edge of the Gulf, and the first sandbar along a beach. It can be a rockpile in the Atlantic surf.

And it can be manmade. In fact, some of the best snook fishing in the state is found in areas that are "spoiled" by development. Residential canals are favorite snook lairs these days. So are the myriad bridges that connect barrier islands to the mainland. Power-plant outflows are great spots for snook in winter, as are ship-turning basins, dredge holes and channels. While none of these areas have made the overall quality of our marine environment any better,

12

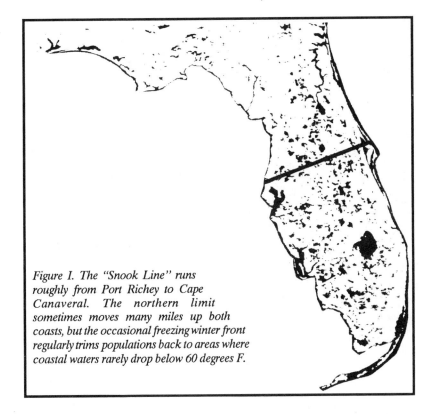

Figure I. The "Snook Line" runs roughly from Port Richey to Cape Canaveral. The northern limit sometimes moves many miles up both coasts, but the occasional freezing winter front regularly trims populations back to areas where coastal waters rarely drop below 60 degrees F.

snook have proven themselves adaptable enough to make use of what civilization gives them.

Because of that, they're a fish for our times. With the proper care and protection, the abundant snook fishing opportunities available today can continue into the next century and beyond, despite the pressures of ever-increasing human populations.

CHAPTER 2

SNOOK COUNTRY

A LOT OF very good snook anglers never bother to look at a nautical chart, on the theory that since they've been fishing their home waters since Eisenhower was in office, there's no need to fool around with some sort of watery map that tells them what they already know. Charts may be needed for long distance navigation, they reason, but not for a Saturday morning trip within five miles of the boat ramp.

But in most cases, even the saltiest of fishermen can learn a few secrets about the areas he fishes, or would fish if he were aware of them, if he studies a recent chart.

This is particularly so for the inshore fisherman, because most coastal areas offer many miles of islands, channels and flats that are all but invisible to those who remain in the marked navigational routes. Unless a talented local shows you his secret trails into the secret spots, they might as well not exist for you.

But with a good chart, you have at your fingertips much of the same information it may have taken the native decades to learn. Nautical charts from N.O.A.A., now about $12 each at chart shops, are among the best investments you can make to improve your fishing and the safety of your navigation.

The charts, made from a combination of aerial photos and marine soundings, show not only all the islands, oyster bars, shoals, tidal rivers and mangrove creeks, they also show the depth of many of those out-of-the-way areas, and even the bottom composition in

Figure 2. Prime snook country like this area east of Marco Island is an archipelago of mangrove islands, shallow bays and deep creeks. Use of a chart is essential to maintain your bearings in such country, and is also a great aid in finding likely snook spots.

most. That composition can often be the tip-off to some prime fishing areas, as well as to safe operation.

Finding Snook Via Charts

You can use a chart to find some pretty good fishing even if you go into an area blind, without any advice from locals. The chart will show water depth in most larger creeks, and anywhere you note good depths of five feet right against the shore approaching a junction of two creeks or a creek and a river, you can bet there will be linesiders hanging around.

Small creeks feeding out of large bays are sure to have fish in

16

Small, mangrove-lined creeks like this one can be snook restaurants on falling tides as baitfish are pulled out of the roots. The angler shown here is David Fairbanks, holder of four world line class records, including the current two-pound record for snook.

them on falling tides because the current there will be intense, pulling the bait out with it. Look particularly for bay mouths with deep cuts in them, six feet or greater, because that indicates the force of the current there has scoured out the area. Strong water flow attracts snook.

Flats and oyster bars sitting across the direction of tide flow are very likely to produce on rising water. The flow will bank bait against the shallows, creating good ambush areas for the snook. There are likely to be eddies where the water falls back to deeper water, and these often produce, as well.

Look for island points with water deeper than three feet against the shore. (Remember, these areas could show as being only one foot deep on the chart, but on a spring tide there may be an added 2 1/2 feet of water there at the peak. Conversely, on the low part of that tide, there won't be any water there--or under your hull--if you stay too long.) When the tide is flowing, these points are likely to produce. So are any potholes near the points.

17

When traveling in remote mangrove country, it's a good idea to frequently look behind as well as ahead, so that you'll better understand what to look for on your return trip. First-timers to the backcountry are smart to mark their progress on a chart so that they can readily return to open water. (Courtesy Aquasport)

Route Your Trips

If you spend a few hours with a red pen (use waterproof ink) circling a series of such spots, you can develop a route for your day on the water that will take advantage of the geography and the changing tide to keep you in likely water all day, perhaps starting around points and flats nearest the open Gulf or Atlantic on a rising tide, and then following the rise inland over several hours to stay on top of the peak water motion where the snook are most likely to be active. On the drop, you'll probably want to be waiting at creek mouths and bay openings for the flush of bait that pours through.

Where ever you go, if you keep an eye on the chart as you travel, you'll have fewer problems with running aground, because you'll always know about how deep the water is ahead of you. (Wear Polarized glasses and keep a sharp lookout, in any case, though. Sometimes the charts don't take into account last year's hurricane that piled up a big shoal where the chart shows four feet of water, and

Charts don't show the tiny potholes that are sometimes snook bonanzas in grass flats. These anglers made use of a tower to locate such a pothole. The elevation makes it easy to see into the water ahead.

sometimes the "mean low tide" reading does not apply when a 20-knot wind blows another six to 12 inches of water seaward.)

Of course, in some areas such as Florida's Everglades, it's foolish to get out of sight of the docks without a chart, because you're almost sure to get lost in the endless mangrove country if you don't keep an eye on the map continuously. First-timers visiting such waters do well to actually draw in their progress, each time they make a major turn, so that they know how to get back out once the mosquito hordes start to fly. On large scale charts, even very small navigational hazards, such as individual submerged pilings and tree stumps, are sometimes indicated--and sometimes these hazards are good spots to cast a live shrimp for a big snook.

Charts are also helpful to inshore anglers who want to locate a spot that's not so easy to find, such as an open water rockpile where fish might gather. You can use the indicated landmarks on the chart, such as water towers or radio beacons ashore, to help you zero in on your spot. Use parallel rules on the chart to get the headings from the landmarks to the fishing spot via the compass rose, then take compass bearings as you fine tune your position.

The one thing charts don't do, yet, is to show individual potholes in the flats where snook might hang out. These holes, often only 10 feet across, are usually too small to show on a chart. But you can draw these in yourself as you learn them, eventually developing a specialized chart that suits your own style of fishing best. (Don't be too sure that those potholes won't show up on charts soon, though. New imaging techniques now in the works show promise of greatly refining depth readings on the next generation of nautical maps.)

Chart Symbols

Some of the chart symbols get very specific, giving you a lot of useful information about bottom conditions. "Rky" for instance, indicates rock bottom. In the right areas, with plenty of tide flow, that sort of bottom will hold snook. "Mud" or "Sft" bottoms, muddy or soft, on the other hand, are less likely to be snook spots--but you can usually jump across shoals with this sort of make-up without danger to your prop, while you can't if the designation is "rky" or "hrd". "Grs" marked in areas from one to five feet deep indicates a grass flat, and if there are channels or blow holes in that flat, there are likely to be snook in them. "Oys" outlined in yellow indicates oyster bars, for which snook have a particular affinity in mangrove country. And a series of curly q's indicates an area where there are strong eddies--often good spots to find gamefish.

Where to Buy Charts

Individual charts are available from map shops and large marinas, or direct from the Distribution Division, NCG/33, National Ocean Survey, Riverdale, MD 20737. You can order by phone and charge it by calling (301) 436-6990. The by-mail price is $13.25 each. If you don't know the number of the charts you might want, you can request a key which shows all those available.

If you fish a lot of different areas and don't want to spring for individual charts of each, you might do well to buy one of the chart books now available. You can save about 80 percent of the cost of buying singles by buying one of the full-size chart books from BBA, Box 407, Needham, Massachusetts 02192. They come about 45 charts to the book, on fold-out, water-resistant paper. Course headings and distance are indicated on commonly traveled routes, and launching areas are pointed out. Whether you go with the book or the singles, keep them dry in plastic envelopes, and store them ashore when not in use, and a set should last you many years. (Don't leave charts or any other paper products aboard--dampness and mildew will do them in.)

Another alternative is the Florida Sportsman Chart Set, which offers the added advantage of having many of the best fishing areas marked by local experts. The charts, about $6 each, cover most of the major fishing areas in snook country. Write to Wickstrom Publishing, 5901 S.W. 74th Street, Miami, Fl 33143 for details.

CHAPTER 3

SNOOK TACKLE

IN THE RIGHT PLACE, you can catch a lunker snook on a rod with all the backbone of a stick of dry spaghetti and line just a bit stronger than sewing thread. Ask David Fairbanks, the man who at this writing holds the 2-pound-test world record for linesiders with a fish that scaled 15-pounds, 4 ounces. Fairbanks, a MirrOlure executive, managed to stick the fish in an open canal with no mangroves or oyster bars near by, and after a 45-minute struggle, he brought it to gaff.

But he figures he lost at least 60 others that were not hooked in the right place and at the right time. In most areas, it takes specialized gear--not 2-pound-test--to consistently bring snook to the boat.

Snook are among the most difficult of all fish to subdue, not only because of their great speed and energy, but also because they are frequently caught in small, snaggly creeks, canals lined with barnacle-encrusted docks, and around the rough cement pilings of bridges and piers. And snook, more than any other species, are completely aware that there is safety in that cover. The first thing most do when they feel the barb is to run as far into the cover as they can. When they get it wrapped over, under, around and through, they grab with both hands and pull. It's over before you can even start to beg.

The time-honored snook rig is a two-handed popping stick around seven feet long and with about as much whip as a curtain rod, rigged with the venerable Ambassadeur 5000 baitcaster. You still

Two-handed baitcasting gear is favored by most experienced snook anglers, like ex-Tampa Bay Bucs footballer Scot Brantley. The rod should be stiff, but light. The revolving spool reel is favored by most snookers because it allows use of heavier line than spinning gear, and is generally more accurate.

Baitcasting reels for snook don't need a huge line capacity. Except for the monsters of the East Coast, it's rare for a snook to run more than 75 yards. Most backcountry anglers choose medium-duty bass type casting reels with free-spool mechanisms for long, accurate casts. The lures shown here, the Bomber Long A (top) and the MirrOlure are two snooking favorites.

see a fair number of these bouncing around the bottom of old aluminum boats with tiller steering, manned by anglers that look like Father Time themselves, and those guys catch snook you'd never imagine.

Modern Baitcasters

But the times have caught up with that tackle. There's better stuff now, and you ought to have it if you're serious about chasing linesiders.

A seven-foot graphite popper like the Series One Berkley B50-7M or similar is hard to beat. These rods are extremely stiff in the lower four-fifths of their length, but taper to a fairly whippy tip that allows casting anything from a 1/8 ounce jig up to a 1-ounce Zara Spook. The feel, in the store before you hang a lure from the end, is about like a fencing rapier, very rigid, with almost none of the whippy

25

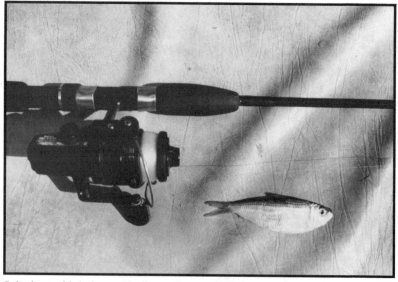

Spinning tackle is favored by those who toss live bait to snook, because it works well with lightweight baits such as Spanish sardines and live shrimp. Spinners work best on the grass flats, where heavy line is not required to hold snook out of the mangroves.

action common in softer graphites or fiberglass rods. These rods are also extremely light, and that's just as important as their strength, because a snook angler may make upwards of 500 casts in a day, and an ounce or two of extra weight can add up over that many throws--especially if you're constantly working the rod on the retrieve as you must with some baits like the Spook.

The old 5000 is superseded by several generations of reels that are a lot easier to cast with, even if they're not, for the most part, as eternally durable. The parent company, Abu-Garcia, still makes some of the best. Shimano, Daiwa and others also produce fine reels. In general, for snooking, you want the free-spool feature and a very dependable and smooth drag, but not much else in the way of bells and whistles. Every extra feature on a reel means more weight and something else that can be ruined by saltwater, sand, or a super-charged fish, so you'll see most of the serious snookers opting for simple, light and strong. A good snook reel, for backcountry casting and most other duties except fishing for the monsters of the piers and bridges, should hold about 120 yards of 14 pound test, and weigh no more than 10 ounces. The 521 XLT Series Ambassadeurs are good, as are most of the Shimano Bantams and the Daiwa Procaster models.

Best line for these reels is 12 to 14 pound test, because it gives smooth casting and adequate strength in most applications. If the fish run big and the cover heavy where you fish, go to 18, but remember you'll sacrifice casting distance and accuracy.

Spinning for Snook

If you just can't master baitcasting, or think you can't, you can catch backcountry snook on spinning gear, but it's going at things the hard way. Spinning gear does not cotton to heavy line unless you use a big, heavy reel to hold it, so that the spool diameter is large enough to allow easy release of the thicker line. But a big, heavy reel is exactly what you don't want for casting in the back country. If you go to a small reel and lighter line that suits it, 8-pound-test or so, you'll break off a lot of lures without ever seeing a snook up close and personal.

On the other hand, if you fish snook on the flats, there's no reason you can't be perfectly happy with spinning gear. In fact, it's the tackle of choice of famed guides like Scott Moore, who catches most of his fish from potholes in open water. The spinning gear is an advantage to live bait anglers in particular, because it's the perfect tool for winging a wiggling sardine out there 150 feet when the wind is blowing straight into your face. You can make the cast into the wind without fear of backlash, and since there's little need for the fine control of accuracy in open water, the spinner has no disadvantages in this application. (I know, some guys are more accurate with spinning gear than 99 percent of us are with baitcasters, but it ain't easy. When you're up against a critter as tough as the snook, why start out standing in a hole?)

The spinning rod for snook on the flats is usually seven feet or longer, because length adds distance, and that's what you need to reach the fish without spooking them in the generally clear waters of the flats. Good graphite sticks for this duty have a stout lower half, to allow authority in pumping in a fish, but the upper half or third is whippy to allow easy casting of live sardines or shrimp. Again, the

27

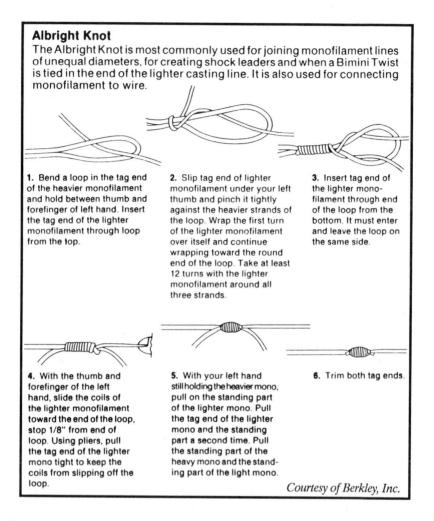

Albright Knot

The Albright Knot is most commonly used for joining monofilament lines of unequal diameters, for creating shock leaders and when a Bimini Twist is tied in the end of the lighter casting line. It is also used for connecting monofilament to wire.

1. Bend a loop in the tag end of the heavier monofilament and hold between thumb and forefinger of left hand. Insert the tag end of the lighter monofilament through loop from the top.

2. Slip tag end of lighter monofilament under your left thumb and pinch it tightly against the heavier strands of the loop. Wrap the first turn of the lighter monofilament over itself and continue wrapping toward the round end of the loop. Take at least 12 turns with the lighter monofilament around all three strands.

3. Insert tag end of the lighter mono-filament through end of the loop from the bottom. It must enter and leave the loop on the same side.

4. With the thumb and forefinger of the left hand, slide the coils of the lighter monofilament toward the end of the loop, stop 1/8" from end of loop. Using pliers, pull the tag end of the lighter mono tight to keep the coils from slipping off the loop.

5. With your left hand still holding the heavier mono, pull on the standing part of the lighter mono. Pull the tag end of the lighter mono and the standing part a second time. Pull the standing part of the heavy mono and the standing part of the light mono.

6. Trim both tag ends.

Courtesy of Berkley, Inc.

entire rod is very light, about the weight you'd use for freshwater bass. If you intend to fish only artificials, you can go with a somewhat stiffer rod. (A good test for either casting or spinning rods to be used in plug casting is to mount a reel on the seat and lean it against the tackle shop wall at about 60-degrees. A rod with adequate backbone for snooking will barely flex in this position.)

The right spinning reels are also light weight, weighing about 10 or 11 ounces. It's not a bad idea to buy a reel designed for 10-pound-test, to give a larger spool for easier casting and smoother drag, but then load it with 8-pound-test so that you can get maximum casting distance. In open water, the light line is adequate to hold even a 20-pounder if you keep the drag light and take your time. Some of the new "long-cast" reels, described elsewhere in this book, are worth consideration, since they add about 10 percent to the casting range of most anglers.

Front-drag reels are smoother than rear drag models, but maybe a little harder to adjust during a fight. There have been advances in rear-drag models in recent years, enough that all of the good ones are adequate for snook fishing.

Pier Gear

For those hearty souls who pursue snook around bridges, piers and docks, forget all the light tackle foolishness recounted above. For this work, you need the biggest, heaviest gear you can heft. The best way is brute force--a 12-foot-long, green Calcutta cane pole, wrapped butt to tip with 100-pound-test mono and with an added yard of line to work the lure, is the most basic and most deadly rig. There's no need for a reel--if the fish runs at all, you've lost him. To this, anglers attach 6/0 forged hooks and live menhaden, 8-inch mullet or ladyfish, or big pinfish. The baits are worked right against the pilings, late on those mosquito-clouded summer nights. When a fish hits, it's *mano e mano* until either man or snook gives. Brutal, but exciting and effective.

Lines for Linesiders

Any quality line will do the job, but in general it's best to stay away from the "high visibility" lines. This stuff really lights up in the bright Florida sun, and when the fish are finicky, as they so often are, you don't want anything to make them suspicious. Clear or pale green is good, or for mangrove-stained water a black line is a good choice. Brands that have lots of followers include Stren, Trilene, Silver Thread and Ande, among many others. There's no need to buy the extreme high-tech stuff made up of "co-polymers" of different kinds of mono, though. You pretty much need to replace snook lines every other day of hard fishing, and at $10 a spool, the co-polymer

The MirrOlure® Knot

This special MirrOlure loop knot is less complicated than most loop knots. It lets your MirrOlure move with a streamlined free and easy action that it is designed for. Your MirrOlure will perform many times better when tied with this simple loop knot.

1. Tie overhand knot loosely in line, then run end of line through screw eye.

2. Pull end through overhand knot parallel with line to rod.

3. Tie a half-hitch on the line toward rod.

4. Pull *both* line and free end tight, forming the loop.

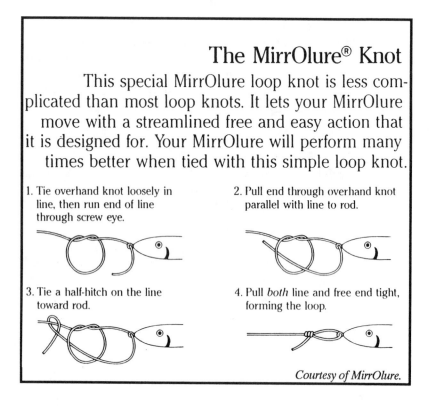

Courtesy of MirrOlure.

lines are too expensive, and no better than any of the quality monos in my experience.

Snook Leaders

Another basic part of snooking gear is the shock leader. It's a piece of heavier mono, about 18 inches long, between lure and line. The purpose is to prevent the sharp gill covers of the snook from cutting through the running line, which it will immediately do if you use line testing less than 15 pounds, and often 15 gets cut, too. You don't want the shock leader to be too heavy, though, because the stiffness and visibility of heavy line will cut down on your strikes. Twenty-five pound test, in a limp mono without a lot of coil or "memory", is a good choice, as is 30 where you expect larger fish and longer battles. During the East Coast mullet run, when 20-pound fish are common, most experts use 40-pound-test for a leader.

The shock leader should be attached to the running line with an Albright Special or a double Uni-knot, rather than a swivel. Even the smallest swivel will catch grass and moss, which reduces strikes. And most of us can't help reeling the swivel through the rod tip occasionally. It doesn't hurt anything going in, but when you cast it back out, it often takes the ceramic eye right out of the tip. With the knot connection, there's nothing to hang on the guides so you can reel the lure in to any distance you want from the tip for most effective and accurate casting.

The lure should be attached to the leader with a loop knot, so that it can swing freely, improving the action. The "MirrOlure Knot" is quick and easy, though it's not so strong as some other knots. But since the loop is being tied in the heavy leader material, a slight loss in strength will make no difference--the knot will still be much stronger than your running line. A Uni-Knot, cinched down with pliers, also works well to create an end loop.

That pretty well covers snooking tackle, except to add that you need at least two of everything for a day in snook country. Rods break, reels jam, lines get terminal backlash. If you can manage to put together two identical outfits, you won't have to shift gears when you go from one to the other. It's not a bad idea to carry a third stick, spinning if you're a baitcaster or vice-versa, so that you can change arms when you get tired. Most anglers work a baitcaster with their left hand, reeling with the right, but work a spinner with the right hand, reeling left. It can give you a new start after four or five hours of working a big topwater plug.

CHAPTER 4

"LIVIES" FOR SNOOK

THERE'S NO MATCH for live bait, year around, for snook fishing. While you can nearly always catch redfish, trout and many other inshore species without ever resorting to anything other than artificials, there are many times when snook simply won't look at anything except the real thing.

There's a lot more to successfully live-baiting snook than buying a bucket of shrimp and anchoring a jumbo out there with an ounce of lead, however. It takes thoughtful, skilled presentations to consistently catch fish, and sometimes it takes more effort to get the bait than it does to catch the snook.

Shrimp for Snook

Shrimp are the easiest live baits to get, and one of the most effective if fished right. To get shrimp most of the year, all you have to do is visit the local bait shop. For starters, always buy "selects" or "jumbos", the largest hand-picked shrimp available. This is not necessarily because snook won't eat small shrimp--they will, with relish. But the larger shrimp survive better, are easier to cast because of their greater weight, and also move around a lot more when hooked, making it more likely they'll attract the eye of a fish.

Shrimp are generally no problem to keep alive in the standard trap-door type ventilated bait bucket, so long as you don't get so many that they're stacked on top of each other. It's better to use a couple of buckets if you get more than two dozen jumbos at a time,

A large cast net and the ability to throw it are basic to successful fishing with many types of live bait. Shrimp, however, can be bought at most bait shops.

to avoid casualties on the way to the water. Keep the buckets in the water anytime the boat is not moving, so that oxygenated water flows through. And in very hot weather, the baits will stay alive better if you set the bucket, half full of water, inside your ice chest. Don't set it directly on or against the ice, but off to one side so that the water is chilled without becoming ice cold. This slows the metabolism of the shrimp, reduces their need for oxygen, and makes them last a lot longer. Or, if you have an aerated bait well in your boat, you can close off the seawater pump, recirculate the water, and float a milk jug full of ice in the well. It will chill the water, but not reduce the brine content as you'd do if you just dumped freshwater ice in there. Shrimp can't stand much fresh water, and can't take any chlorine, which commercial ice frequently contains.

And if you're going on a long trip where you won't have access to fresh shrimp for a while, as you might in a houseboat trip into the Everglades, you can keep shrimp alive for up to a week by putting them in alternating layers of wet newspaper and ice in an ice chest. These shrimp won't ever come back to life enough to swim actively, but they'll still be completely fresh and make excellent cut bait for tipping jigs. They can also be fished whole on a shrimp harness.

Shrimp Tackle

Some folks use entirely too much tackle for effectively fishing a shrimp. Think of it as casting a live butterfly and you'll start to tune your gear properly. A shrimp is a light, delicate creature, and in order to look anything like its free-swimming cousins, the one on your line is going to have to carry very little weight along with him. The 5/0 forged hook that you might like for fishing live pinfish in the passes just won't work for shrimp. Its large diameter will crack the shell, and probably kill the bait immediately, and the extra weight will drag the shrimp to bottom, rather than allowing it to flutter and flip along in mid-water or at the surface in the way that drives snook nuts.

Instead, you want a light-weight hook, fine wire, no larger than 2/0, with a small barb that won't poke a big hole in the shrimp's shell and let out the watery fluid that passes for blood in this unique creature. In fact, you may want to flatten the barb of your hook, as well as touching up the point with a hone, so that it goes through the shell as smoothly as possible. (A hook treated this way will also hook fish more easily, as you might expect. It won't come out if you keep steady pressure on the line. And it's much easier to remove once the fish is landed, an important consideration in these days of catch-and-release fishing.)

Aha! But won't the light hook bend out straight when I hook a big fish, you ask?

It could happen, true.

But in general, you have to fish shrimp on light spinning gear anyway, so that you can get reasonable casting distance. This means you're going to be limited to line no heavier than 10 pound test (8 is a better choice in most water), and when you set your drag light enough to avoid breaking these light lines, it won't be tight enough to bend out the light hooks. Just don't grab the shock leader and try to lift the fish that way, because the hook will straighten under that sort of pressure. Use a net, or grab the fish's jaw, or beach it if you're fishing from shore.

The best way to fish live shrimp is usually unweighted or "free-lined" on spinning gear and a lightweight hook. The unweighted bait allows a very natural presentation. Snook don't readily take a shrimp anchored to bottom by a heavy lead.

(Incidentally, the fine wire hooks, sharpened and with the barb bent down, are particularly helpful when fishing with light mono. The light stuff stretches a lot, so there's very little force exerted when you jerk on the rod. With the small point diameter of the fine wire, you stand a much better chance of getting a solid hookup.)

Shrimp are best fished either free-lined, with nothing on the line but the hook and shock leader, or about three feet under a popping cork. In either case, you don't cast it out and forget it. The idea is to fish the bait much like you would an artificial, casting it so that it drifts past those swirly points and over those yellow sand holes and underneath those overhanging mangroves. You fish it with the flow of the tide, and when it drifts out of the likely area, you crank it back and throw again. A shrimp left trailing from a rod in a holder does not look lifelike at all, and though you'll occasionally catch the local suicide, consistent results depends on keeping the bait moving naturally through the strike zones.

How you place the hook depends on the water you're fishing. For shallow flats and moving water, placing the hook just under the horn at the front of the shell is usually best. Turn the hook sideways when you insert it, so that the hump on the barb does not cut through the horn, and the bait will stay on the hook better. Be sure not to put the hook too low, where it will hit the heart or other vitals--just slip it under the horn, and it will hold until a fish finds him.

Sometimes you'll be fishing in an area where you really don't want the shrimp to swim much, such as overhanging mangroves where the bait will snag if it moves much at all. In those areas, you might prefer to hook the shrimp through the last joint of the tail. This will restrict his swimming motion considerably, and hopefully keep you out of the snags. The tail hook-up also is a bit stronger than hooking under the horn, so you may want to try it when you have to make an exceptionally long cast where the force might rip the shell in the front-end hookup.

For very long casts, it's sometimes necessary to bury the whole hook in the bait, as bonefish anglers do on the flats of the keys. You run it in at the tail, out just under the carapace. This kills the shrimp, but if you work it slowly and patiently, the snook don't seem to notice. (It's a good idea to break off the flat part of the tail when you fish this way, both to prevent the bait from spinning and to put a bit of scent into the water.)

Another alternative rig is the shrimp harness, such as those from Pico and other manufacturers. These are spring-loaded devices that clamp over the horn and the shell, cradling the bait against a hook without ever penetrating any part of the shell or body. Survival is good, and the presentation is very natural.

Fresh shrimp also make great tipping baits for jigs, of course. Just be sure to use the minimum that will stay on the hook. You want a piece no larger than a pencil eraser, just enough to add a bit of scent without changing the shape or action of the lure. Use only the tail section, and cut it so that each chunk has a surrounding layer of shell, which will help it stay on the hook.

Catching and Fishing Sardines

For a lot of snook fishermen, the only "baitfish" that counts is the Spanish sardine. This flat-sided, shad-like fish averages about 3 to 4 inches long, and can be found over the grass flats around passes throughout the spring, summer and fall on both coasts. It's easily

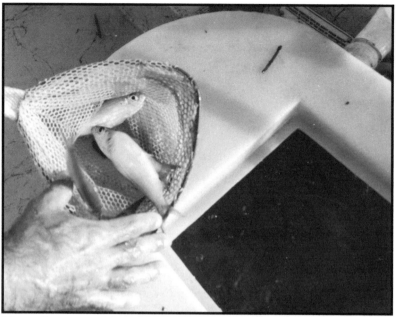

Live sardines are worth their weight in silver to snook anglers. They are the ultimate bait for almost assured catches. But they're sometimes tough to find, and they're always tough to keep alive in a bait well. Most anglers find it necessary to catch their bait daily, usually by chumming with canned mackerel and bread over the grass flats.

chummed into cast-net range with a mix of whole wheat bread and canned jack mackerel, and some aficionados like nationally-known snook guide Scott Moore, refine the mix by adding anise oil and canned sardines. In any case, when you net up a well full of these flashing, fidgeting minnows, you've all but guaranteed yourself a day of hot snook action. The fabulous trips that make the newspapers, 30, 40 and even 50 snook a day, are nearly all the result of fishing live sardines.

The baits must be kept in a large live well with rounded corners, and with a powerful and continuous flow of seawater coming in, waste water going out. They live only a few minutes without the continuing circulation.

Sardines are fished much the same way as the shrimp. They're light, and they're delicate, and they do best on light hooks, though they can carry a somewhat more substantial hook than a shrimp without being weighted down. A 2/0 Sproat is a good choice, and again, it's a good idea to flatten the barb and sharpen the point.

Sardines have a soft, clear spot in their nose, just below the eyes, that looks as if it was designed as the place to put a hook. Hooked through that spot, they stay alive well and are extremely active, and they stay on the hook during a long cast--a problem if you hook them in the lips or back.

Sardine tackle, again, is light weight. A 7-foot (or longer) spinning rod with a soft tip, line testing no more than 10 pounds, and an open faced spinning reel is the ticket. Guides who use the sardines daily--guys like Scott Moore and James Wood, both from the Cortez area--use custom built rods 8 1/2 feet long to allow them to really whip the baits a mile.

The sardines work best in the shallows, around holes in the grass flats, island points, shell bars and the like. They're fished unweighted, and allowed to swim where ever they want. They're strong swimmers, and will cover a lot of water, doing the scouting for you. And when they see a snook, they let you know by coming up on top, swimming madly and sometimes splashing around like a Bangolure on autopilot. When you see that, hang on, because an explosion is imminent.

Most expert sardine anglers believe in chumming likely holes with loose baits, particularly those that are a bit gimpy and will flutter and wobble on top when they land. After the fish start eating the free ones, the one with the hook goes to the same spot, usually to a resounding welcome.

Pinfish - Durable and Abundant

Pinfish are also a good snook bait, though more because they're easy to catch (either chummed up and castnetted or via number 10 hooks and bits of shrimp) and hardy on the hook than because they're a preferred snook food. It's likely that the spines which earn pins their name don't particularly appeal to snook, and if they could have their druthers they'd definitely rather have a nice, soft sardine, but when you wave a struggling pinfish in their face long enough, something usually happens.

Pins are a common bait for drifting the deeper passes in spring,

39

and they do a good job in this situation because it's essential to put on plenty of weight to get the bait down near bottom, in strong tides, in water up to 20 feet deep. They're strong swimmers and can entertain an approaching snook despite the weight, which a lot of other baits don't under these conditions.

Pins also catch plenty of big snook off docks, piers and bridges. In these situations, you need very heavy tackle, 5/0 forged hooks, and lines testing 20 pounds and right on up to the hundred-pound-test jigger pole stuff, to manhandle a big fish away from the pilings. Wimpy baits just can't carry the hardware, so a spunky, stout little critter like the pinfish is the better choice. They can be hooked through the flexible part of both lips, in the fleshy part of the head, in the back just under the dorsal, or in the upper part of the tail. They're easy to keep alive, even in a small bait bucket, if the water is changed regularly and they don't get too warm.

Other Baitfish That Snook Love

Tilapia, the African invaders which have escaped into so much of the fresh and brackish water throughout the southern half of Florida, are also excellent snook bait, in sizes up to about 6 inches long. They're very hardy on the hook, active, and fairly easy to catch by castnetting weedy shallows of coastal rivers. Don't move them from one watershed to another, though. Even though they're already in most systems, it's dumb, and illegal, to help them spread.

Mullet, ladyfish, silver trout and a variety of other species also make good snook baits at times. Finger mullet are a particular favorite along the East Coast, but not often used on the west side for some reason. They're strong, active baits, and come in sizes big enough to challenge even a 30-pound linesider. They're fairly delicate in captivity, and like sardines, require lots of fresh seawater boiling through a big live well at all times. They can handle heavy hooks and line and stay active, and are among the favored baits of the few anglers who specialize only in monster snook around East Coast passes and bridges. Particularly when the mullet run is on in October, a struggling 8-incher swum in the slough of the surf or around the pass jetties is dynamite.

It's usually no problem to catch all the mullet you want during the mullet run, either by flicking a cast net over them as they ease

A variety of small fish work as snook bait. Ladyfish, mullet, silver trout and tilapia, shown here, are all effective. The tilapia, exotics imported by the aquarium trade, are found in many coastal rivers of Florida these days. They're legal to use as bait, but should not be moved from watershed to another.

along the surface, or by snatch-hooking one with a large treble. If you catch them with a net, you'll have to let most of them go, because you can't keep many alive at once even in a sizable livewell. And in the five-gallon can most beach anglers carry, only a couple of spares can be kept kicking. Considering how easy it is to get more, there's no reason to net a large number at once, in any case, and the fresher the mullet, the better they swim.

The hook is put through the lips, or sometimes just behind the tail fin, and the mullet is cast right back to the swash channel, but a bit to the outside of the main mullet school. Snook seem to constantly dog the migrating baits, always looking for a weak one like wolves following caribou. They'll rush the bait pods, sending the mullet scattering in all directions as they look for a slow one. The one with the hook in it usually turns out to be slowest, and BANG, you're in business.

If no fish are rushing the schools, you can often draw a strike by tail-hooking a bait, casting it to the outer edge of the slough, and then pulling it up on the surface with slight backward pressure, making it flutter and splash on top. It draws some outrageous hits.

This sort of fishing takes stout gear, because the baits are heavy and hard to handle on light stuff, and also because a 25-pound snook just might swim off with all your line if you're fishing a bass-sized baitcaster loaded with 10-pound test. It's better to go with something

41

like an Ambassadeur 7000 loaded with 20 on a stout seven to eight foot rod. And if there are tarpon in the area, which there frequently are during the peak of the run, you might move on up to something like a Penn 209 loaded with 30.

Mullet are also great baits in inside waters, though not many anglers take the time to capture them and fish them properly. For those who do, again selecting baits six to nine inches long and fishing them on stout gear, the rewards can be giant fish in areas where not many people expect them. The mouths of residential canals and the bridge pilings throughout the Miami area are noted for producing monsters to this type of approach by experts like Al Pflueger, Jr.

With a bit of practice, you can learn to "steer" a tail-hooked mullet right in among the pilings, where he'll flip and flash until the fish can't stand it. Getting the snook out once it takes is another matter, however. The only solution is for you to go to the fish, threading the line around the bridge supports without pulling on it hard enough to saw through on the barnacles. You still lose a lot of fish, but you land some, too. Heavy line is a must, with 30-pound the minimum, 40 much better.

Not many people try it, but old Crackers know that snook are not above taking cut mullet on occasion, just like tarpon. The mullet has to be fresh, and it can't be washed out by extended use. But a strip about two inches wide and six inches long, fished on a 4/0 hook and allowed to drift with the current along cut banks and deep points will often connect when you can't get hold of any live baits to do the job.

Ladyfish, silver trout, spotted trout and many other species are also snook fodder, but these are all baits of opportunity rather than something you can fill a livewell with and go off in pursuit of snook. However, if you catch a 12-inch ladyfish around a dock or ocean pier at night (shrimp, small jigs and spoons do the job) and trail it around the pilings on a 5/0 forged hook, Calcutta pole and line better suited to tripping steers, you will get some astonishing strikes.

Crabs are also a very good snook bait, and in some areas it's rare to open a snook stomach without finding the remains of crab shells inside. Fiddlers are good and easy to catch in estuarine areas on low water. So are the small "dollar" crabs, no more than three inches across the shell, like those used for tarpon at Boca Grande. They're hardy in a cool bucket of saltwater and moss, stay alive on the hook indefinitely, and can't be stolen by pinfish. Snook don't take them as rapidly as they'll take sardines or shrimp, in my experience, but when you can't get either, crabs may be the way to go. It takes a stout, sharp hook to penetrate the shells, a 2/0 strong or the like, and you may want to file the point a bit after you put it through. After that, though, you can stop worrying about the bait until something eats it. A single crab will last for hours on the hook, if a snook doesn't find him. No live bait will last so long as an artificial, of course, but they don't have to. Livies are so deadly that their life expectancy is usually limited to one cast.

CHAPTER 5

SKIPPIN' AND POPPIN' AND MANGROVE MIGRAINES

SCIENTISTS REMAIN AMBIGUOUS on whether it's possible for a mangrove to reach out and grab a snook plug.

But personally, I'm convinced. I've seen them do it many times.

In fact, I suspect that the mangrove was genetically engineered by a crazed snook-plug manufacturer, for the express purpose of maximizing his sales. That's the only explanation of a tree that grows with its twisting, tangling, blankety-blanking roots sticking up in the air, instead of down in the ground where all respectable plants keep their privates.

Those roots are designed like Velcro, with millions of microscopic little hooks bio-engineered to perfectly fit the hooks on your plugs. Whenever the plant sees one pass close by, up go the roots, shooting out like the tongue of a giant frog, and snatch goes your $5.95 lure.

Did you ever notice how the thickest stands are always planted right over the best holes? You can't tell me somebody didn't put them there. Either that, or they grow each time they eat a plug. Do MirrOlures make good mangrove fertilizer? They're still doing the research on it.

Be all that as it may, not only snook but also a lot of other species of Southern fish love mangroves. Redfish and sheepshead are regular patrons of mangrove mazes, as are, obviously, mangrove snapper.

Extracting these creatures from the living fingers of the obstinate botanicals, however, takes some doing.

Mangroves have a remarkable--and maddening--capability to reach out and snatch artificial lures. Snook spend much of their juvenile lives within the root jungles, and even when full-grown, they continue to hang close to the dense cover, using it for shade and for ambush. (Courtesy Outboard Marine Corporation.)

The problems begin with getting the lure into the overhung hidey-holes where the fish lie. Most productive mangrove shorelines are along channels and creeks, where deep, flowing water goes right up to the bank. As the limbs spread, competing for the sunlight over the open water, they reach out far from the actual shoreline to create a sort of artificial shore that may be 10 or 15 feet from the real edge.

Guess where the fish are?

Yep. They never see the light of day.

Mangrove migraines. A narrowing of the vision, and a feeling you're looking through a tunnel. Intense headaches. Vertigo.

The fish prowl in there, sucking crabs and killifish and other small edibles out of the roots. They're usually looking toward the shore, or parallel to it, rather than out toward open water. So that's where your lure needs to get in order for many of them to notice it.

In order to make the presentation, you've got to be an angling magician, capable of making your lure materialize in spots with about as much space as there is under the average living room couch. It's impossible. And to make things worse, those big old hawg snook and yard-long reds like to get back in there and wallow and root and blow bait out on the bank, just to tease you.

It's enough to make you take up golf.

However, where there's a will, there are greedy relatives. No--there's a way.

In this case, it's skippin'. Or poppin'.

Skip Your Lure to the Fish

Skippin' is my own adaption of the bass angler's "flippin'", which is either (a.) a small town in Arkansas surrounded by a large bass boat factory, or (b.) a method of catching bass in heavy cover without the use of dynamite.

Skippin' is different from dippin', which is done to snuff by Southern anglers, and from sippin', which is done to whiskey by said fishermen as a cure for mangrove migraine.

It's a method of getting the lure to the fish under the spreading mangrove trees.

It's not really new--what is?--but it's been pretty much forgotten by most Florida fishermen, who are the primary practitioners of mangrove fishing, since they have the great majority of the nation's mangroves along their shorelines.

Skippin' has a lot in common with the trick you used to do as a kid with a flat stone. If you throw a flat object parallel to the water and very hard, it hydro-planes along the surface in a series of skips instead of plummeting downward.

Old-time snook anglers in the 10,000 Islands area started applying the idea to spoons in the 1950's. With a powerful sidearm cast, they learned they could skip a lure well back under the overhang, and often connect with some prodigious fish.

Skippin' Live Baits

The idea still works just as well today, and a few fishermen such as guide Chris Mitchell of Boca Grande are rediscovering it.

On a recent trip, Mitchell and I skipped not lures, but live sardines, to a horde of hungry snook burrowed into the mangroves of Charlotte Harbor, on the west coast near Fort Myers. Sardines are flat sided, smooth, and just the right weight for skippin', and Mitchell has become a master at it.

The baits are hooked through the nose with a 1/0 hook, rigged on a couple feet of 30-pound-test shock leader. The heavy leader is essential to prevent cutoffs on the sharp gill covers of a snook. The bait is cast, unweighted, on a 7-foot, two-handed spinning rod and open faced reel, spooled with 8 to 10 pound test.

Mitchell winds up and drives the baits toward the cover with a mighty snap of both wrists, which sends the wide-eyed minnow zipping along in a trajectory about like that of a .30-06, just off the water. At the point where the tree limbs begin, it touches down, then goes skipping far back underneath in a series of short hops. Once it lands at last, the amazed minnow goes poking off into the roots, and usually runs into real trouble in short order.

Mitchell says he uses the spinning rigs because the completely free line whispering off the fixed spool creates no drag, and doesn't backlash when the bait starts to skip. With a baitcaster, as you thumb the revolving spool you either stop the skipping altogether, or you get a monumental backlash when the bait starts to skip.

As you might expect, sometimes the minnow lands in the trees, where it catches plenty of blue herons if you're not quick about it. And because of the rough handling, even those that land where you want them are only good for a couple of casts. So you need plenty. (Mitchell gets extra to chum with, too. He likes to "sweeten" a hole by throwing free sardines into it first. When half-a-dozen are spinning around under the limbs, he puts in the one with the hook on it, usually to an explosive welcome.)

Speaking of catching birds, the live baits do present somewhat of a problem in that direction. If you break any baits off in the trees, conservation and simple ethics says you've got to go and retrieve hook, line and bait so that they don't become a death trap for the many birds that use this cover for roosting and feeding.

Spinning gear is favored for "skippin'" baits under the mangroves, because backlash is not a problem. However, the light line required for spinning reels can make it difficult to extract a big snook like this one from the cover.

Skippin' Artificials

With artificial lures, you don't have to worry so much about roughing the baits, and most people can cast further and more accurately with a spoon than with a sardine. The time-honored lure for the technique is the Johnson Silver Minnow, a single-hook spoon with a wire weedguard, and with most of the weight concentrated at the bottom, the end away from the eyelet. The half-ounce size in gold finish is a Florida favorite.

With practice, you can rifle this lure a hundred feet and send it skipping another 10 with no problem. The secret is in keeping the rod tip low to the water as you make the cast, and driving hard on the forward stroke. The lure should never rise more than three feet above the water in its flight. If you throw a higher arc, it will tend to catch the limbs as it falls, and also will tend to sink instead of skip.

The skipping, in addition to getting your offering into the strike zone, also adds an extra dimension of flash and splash and action that seems to turn on the fish. Many times the strike comes the instant the bait or lure settles into the water. And in a few cases, a fish will actually pick it off while it's still hopping along the top--sort of a reflex strike, apparently.

There are some other lures that also work in skippin'. The Zara Spook is fair, due to its smooth, torpedo like body--though with all the treble hooks, it's highly susceptible if any of those moving

49

mangrove roots are around. Other excellent snook plugs like the Bang-o-lure and both the floating and slow-sink MirrOlures don't skip very well, but you can sidearm them in there close enough to stir things up a lot of times. With floating plugs, sometimes you can let the current help you out, casting as close as you can upcurrent and then free-lining to let the tide float the lure back in before you start to work it.

Poppin' The Mangroves

Finally, if you're insistent on ferreting out every last critter hiding in the tangles, you can try poppin' them out. This is a better-known technique employing the popping cork, but most anglers practice it in open water. It works there, of course. But it's also an effective way to pull fish out from under cover where you otherwise can't get to them, not even by skippin'.

The technique is generally used with live bait, the above-mentioned live sardines, or small pinfish or jumbo shrimp. (If you're after meat in the pot, opt for the shrimp--you'll catch lots of sheepshead, snapper and drum in addition to the snook and reds.)

These are fished on 1/0 hooks, unweighted, rigged on 3-foot shock leaders of 30-pound test. The popping cork is mounted on the upper end of the shock leader, not on the running line. The crimping of light line with the stopper stick is enough to weaken it and cause a break-off, but won't hurt the heavier leader material--and the cork will stay put better when fastened on the larger diameter mono, too.

The rig is cast as close to the mangroves as you dare, and then jerked and gurgled and pulled until it sounds like a plumber's helper gone mad.

The fish, back under the protective limbs, hear all the fuss, which to them approximates the noise made by a school of trout or jacks in a feeding orgy. They swim out to investigate, see the bait, and gulp it, according to the plan.

The same technique works well if you hang a 1/8 to 1/4 oz. plastic-tailed jig or bucktail on the leader. The jerks of the cork make it rise in the water, then plunge back toward bottom. The trouble most folks have with fishing a popping cork is that it's difficult to set the hook. The reason is that the cork, following a running fish, creates a couple feet of slack between itself and the hook. So unless you use a stout rod and set on a tight line with plenty of authority, you won't drive the barb home. Wimpy rods and limp wrists won't get it. Once you connect with a big fish around the mangroves, you may find the migraines really begin. Snook, in particular, are noted for swimming back in and crawling out on the bank the minute they feel the steel. You'll lose plenty of fish and plenty of tackle, no matter what you do. But sometimes if you're careful and patient, you can sort out seemingly hopeless situations.

As soon as you feel or see the line go around a oyster-encrusted root, the only recourse is to put the reel in free-spool. If you don't, the battle is over because the line will be cut instantly. So long as you're still connected, there's hope.

The trick is to follow the line, poling the boat after it and carefully separating it from the limbs and roots as you go. (Yes, the mosquitoes and no-see-ums will be waiting for you. Yes, there are sometimes snakes in those roots. You're here to fish, not to have a good time. Remember that.)

A fair number of times you'll come on the fish, way back there in a foot of water, resting in what he thinks is his safe house. If you reach out with a long-handled net, you can sometimes capture the fish before it gets suspicious.

True, a lot of times you won't.

But, hey, you were going to release him anyway.

Weren't you?

A few years back I was fishing with Karl Wickstrom, publisher of Florida Sportsman Magazine, and his wife Sheila, near the mouth of the Shark River in the Everglades when Sheila hooked a big snook right next to an undercut mangrove island. The fish did the predictable thing, and zipped right up under the bank.

All of us had been in the plight often enough to know that we couldn't pull the fish out by force, so we decided to wait him out.

Our patience lasted about 15 minutes, during which time the snook, chewing thoughtfully on the shrimp, decided it was doing just fine exactly where it was.

We had a pushpole aboard, and I opined that maybe we could use it to give the snook a push.

We eased in close, carefully threading the line around the overhanging roots. When we had gone as far as we could, I slid the pole down beside the line and began probing. I could feel it crunching against barnacles and oysters up in there, and eventually, I tapped something that tapped back.

The snook shot out of the roots like a cake of soap squirting from a wet hand. He ran straight to the middle of the river, and that's where the battle ended. He had no inclination to go back into the mangroves and tangle with whatever it was that had slithered up on him.

The trick worked in part because Sheila was fishing fairly stout line, as I recall, 15-pound-test or thereabout, which allowed it to touch the shells without being snipped.

But a year ago at Pine Island Sound, I didn't have such good luck with lighter line. I was pitching a Bangolure on a grass flat for trout among the inside islands, fishing the lure on a spinning rig and 6-pound mono, when I drifted past a mangrove point. Couldn't resist a toss over there, even though I knew it was risky with the light tackle.

Sure enough, a linesider about the length of my leg rolled up and BALOOPed it down. The fish zipped out into the center of the flat and stuck it's head out, and things were going just fine. But then it saw the boat, and decided it was time to exit, and ran right for the tree-line.

I put a finger on the spool and pressured it all I dared, but the fish seemed not to notice. When he got to the first limbs, I could see it was no use, so I dropped the tip to get a bit of slack and opened the bail.

The fish stayed connected, but he didn't stop swimming until he was way back under the overhanging limbs. I ran the boat over there and tried to sort it out, and I finally could see him laying back almost against the shore in a little shell pocket between the roots.

Dipped and twisted and jockeyed the rod, and finally figured I had all the line free, and raised up on it just a bit to see if I could steer him clear.

One little shell, hanging off a root just above the shock leader, was the only thing that touched that line. But it was enough. It parted.

I stepped down among the roots and tried to get him anyway, but the second I got within reaching distance, he went back out the way he had come and that was that.

Hey, I really would have let him go, anyway.

CHAPTER 6

WADING THE FLATS

SNOOK AREN'T SO dumb as they used to be. The boom in flats fishing in recent years has made the "big game" of the shallows a lot more savvy than they were in the days before everyone had a boat that would float in ankle-deep water--and knew there were fish to go after in water that shallow.

By now, everybody has pretty well learned that you don't run your outboard on the flats anywhere within a couple hundred yards of where you hope to fish, and more and more anglers are even getting nervous about turning on the trolling motor anywhere near their alleged honey hole. Like bonefish, it seems that some hard-fished and often-released snook will shut down if they hear the whir of an electric getting a bit too close, and that goes double for big fish that have been around awhile. Maybe their extra caution is the reason they get big, just like big whitetail bucks.

Poling is all but silent, of course, but you pretty much need to be up on a platform to do it. And fish, like deer, are learning to look up for danger. They know you aren't a great blue heron with a cane, up there leaning on that pole, no matter how innocent you try to look. While it's true that the higher up you get, the better you can see into the water, it's also true that the higher up you get, the better the fish can see you.

The answer, of course, is to get out of the boat.

I know, you paid 20 grand to buy that high-tech, foam-cored, 600-pound wonder, and you want to fish up on the nice, clean, non-skid decks, not down there in the mud and sting rays.

Many anglers use a shallow-draft boat to reach remote fishing areas, then go over the side for a silent, low-profile approach to snook hotspots that may be only knee-deep.

But sometimes, it's the only way.

For starters, it eliminates all noise. No growling outboard, no whirring electric, no crunching push pole, no slap of waves against the hull, no dropped drink cans. That alone can add several fish daily to your take.

Second, and maybe most important, wading greatly reduces your silhouette. A man standing waist-deep is no more alarming than a mangrove snag to a fish. Compare that to the broad, white hull of the typical flats boat, catching light reflected from bottom and sending out a glow in all directions, plus the far taller above-water structures, and you can readily understand why it's no problem for a wade fishermen to best a boat fisherman a lot of the time.

Wading - The Subtle Approach

Richard Seward, a noted Tampa Bay snook expert, gets results by wading many shallow flats around the bay area. Seward often fishes "swash channels" that most other anglers don't even know exist. He's able to find them only because he wades.

"The "channel" may only be 8 inches or a foot deeper than the surrounding water," says Seward. "You can't see that difference from a boat or read it on a depth recorder, but you can easily pick it out if you're wading. When the water goes out, the fish will find it, and if you're there, in the water where they aren't going to see you, you can catch a load of fish where most other people would never even make a cast."

Wading is particularly useful on those breathless days when you can see a dollar crab surface a hundred yards away. A flat surface and clear water make it very tough to sneak within casting range in a boat. Even wading, you spook some fish under these conditions, but it's not nearly as bad as from the boat.

Wade to Secret Spots

You can also access some areas wading that you just can't get at afloat. Those neat little back country potholes and creeks, often guarded by an oyster bar that comes through the surface at half-tide, offer tremendous action at times in fall and winter, but you have to get into the water to reach them. After you crunch across the bar (make certain to wear hard-soled shoes or you'll be sorry!) you've literally got the fish surrounded. If you don't spook them, you can work on them until the tide returns--they're not going anywhere, and nobody else is going to bother them.

Dress for Wading

Speaking of shoes, finding the right footwear for wading is a major part of making it enjoyable. Conventional low-rise sneakers constantly fill up with sand and grit, which can drive you nuts with chafing after a few hours. Socks help, but not much. High top sneakers are a better choice, and best of all are divers' boots, which fit snugly around the ankles and keep all debris out, yet are tough enough to ward off the cuts and scrapes common in wading. There are now also some wading shoes aimed at the saltwater wade fishermen-Omega's Reef Warriors are good ones, among others.

If you wade all day long, it's a good idea to wear light cotton or nylon slacks, rather than shorts. Otherwise, you're likely to get a sunburn on your legs, because few sun screens will stay on long in the water.

A fishing vest is a big help, too, because you always need a lot of stuff like pliers and extra shock leader and lures that you can't carry in pants pockets. Make sure you don't carry anything that will rust or corrode in the salt water, and that includes your car keys.

As the water cools in fall and winter, wade fishing continues to be effective, but you need to add chest waders to your gear. Best are the neoprene jobs, because they're light and flexible. The heavy-duty Cordura nylon models will last forever, though they're bulky.

Where and When to Wade

Wading works best if you use it as a spot fishing technique, rather than a general, all-day tool. The reason, of course, is that you don't cover much ground while wading. While you may catch every fish that's near you, there may not be any near you if you start in the wrong spot. So the best technique is to start in the boat and drift, pole, or idle across likely water--grass flats from 2 to 6 feet deep-- looking for fish. You can soon learn to pick out the dark shadows created by fleeing snook, especially if you watch for them on patches of bare sand that show up as yellow spots wherever the water has the slight tinge common in mangrove country. Snook look like gray-brown torpedoes as they ease over these spots, with their back humped and their nose more pointed than that of the redfish. You can often see the line down their sides, too

Though you will "blow out" fish from the holes as you pass near them in a boat, if you wait 20 minutes, they'll often return. And after you note the kinds of areas that are holding fish on a given day, you can often predict other spots that will also produce due to similar conditions. On rising water, for example, you may want to find a mangrove shoreline with grass abutting. On the fall, you might look for holes near points, where eddies will form, or perhaps channel edges and bay outflows.

Remember, if you're wading on a rising tide, that the water that was chest deep when you crossed that channel will be over your head when you come back. Remember it especially if you can't swim. And if you go a long way downtide on a deep flat, you'll find it very hard

Because wading rarely spooks fish, it's especially effective when a sizable school of snook is located in a pothole in shallow flats. Because waders don't cover a lot of water, it's not a good scouting technique.

to return while the flow is still strong against you--keep it in mind if dark is coming and you don't like 'skeeters. One of the best ways to wade fish is with a partner, who parks the boat a couple hundred yards in front of you, then wades forward until you get to the boat to leapfrog past him. That way, your extra gear and cold drinks are never too far off, and you don't have far to wade when you're ready to quit.

Even when wading, it's essential to remember that you don't want to make a lot of commotion. Move slowly, keep your rod low to the water, and don't move at all when fish come close following your lure.

And though white clothes are most comfortable in hot, sunny weather, darker shades are less visible to the fish and less unnatural in the usual mangrove environment. One of the nice things about wading, of course, is that it keeps you cool when summer temperatures soar. Don't be afraid to crouch down now and then and wet your shirt, so that evaporation will help things along. (Again, don't carry stuff that can't stand saltwater unless you carry it in sealed Ziplock style bags. Even if you don't get in deep enough to wet it, water has a way of creeping up your clothing to wet stuff like cigarettes and film).

Flyrodding and wade fishing were made for each other, because when you're in the water, there's nothing for the extra coils of line to tangle with, and nothing for the backcast to snag.

Also, because of the low profile, you don't need to make hundred-foot casts (which most of us can't do anyway) to reach the fish.

In fact, there will be times when you can simply "dabble" the fly out there just beyond rod's length and connect, though that more often works with near-sighted redfish than with the more visually alert snook.

However, if you can throw 50 feet, and just about anyone can if they don't have a boat getting in the way, you can catch a snook while wading with the fly.

The soft presentation possible with the flyrod makes it particularly suited for use in the extreme shallows where wading is the only reasonable approach, too. Many times, a streamer or a popper settling to the water triggers an immediate strike when put a couple yards ahead of a fish that's cruising along in a foot of water, while if you dropped a big Zara Spook in next to him, he'd jump out of his skin. The streamers also allow a slow-sinking presentation that won't foul bottom weeds like treble-hooked lures or lead-head jigs will. And, it allows you to fish quarter-sized epoxy crabs that look almost identical to the real thing. When snook are prowling shallow, they're prowling for crustaceans, and they won't often turn down the crab. (Ocean Flies at Crystal River (904) 895-9080, makes some great ones.)

Dangers Few, But Real

Wherever you wade, it's essential to keep your eyes open for sting rays. They'll get out of your way if they have the chance, but you've got to move slowly and slide your feet so that they can cooperate. Sharks? No problem, in the back country. You might see one now and then, but they're generally too small to be of any concern. Nearer open water, a sizable blacktip might make you nervous now and then, especially if you hang a stringer of fish on your belt, but in general, wading in clear water presents almost zero danger from "Jaws".

CHAPTER 7

FINE AND FAR AWAY

SOME 200 YEARS AGO, Izaac Walton admonished his readers that at times it was necessary to fish "fine and far away". That advice, originally fashioned for finicky fresh water trout, is becoming appropriate for the inshore saltwater angler as the pressure on flats species grows, and the fish become ever more wary of the wiles of anglers.

The idea, of course, is to get the bait or lure to the fish accurately, without giving it an inkling that you're around. And that sometimes means fishing lighter lines than many of us are used to spooling, and making casts farther than we are generally capable of making.

Bonefish anglers in the Florida Keys have long had the problem to deal with, because bones have long been a target of skilled light-tackle addicts, and because they're found in knee-deep water that's often nearly air-clear. Keys bonefish are smart and spooky as a result, and most anglers know that it takes both skill and special gear to pursue them.

But the same thing is gradually becoming true for snook, as well as reds and trout found on the flats in waters like the shoals of Charlotte Harbor, Tampa Bay and Biscayne Bay. It's less applicable in murky waters like those of the Everglades mangrove country, where a short, accurate cast is usually the order of the day, but even there, there are spots where being able to really whale one out there makes the difference between success and failure.

Guide Paul Hawkins, who fishes many flats within sight of the busy skyline of St. Petersburg, FL, deals with fish that see lots of lures every day, in water so clear that you can watch a crab scuttle along bottom in five feet. His solution is two-fold: first, he gets out of the boat, thus cutting both the height and the cross-section presented to the fish. And secondly, he uses two-handed rods and takes advantage of the wind to send out long casts that help him make certain the fish see the lure before they sense the fishermen.

"Anymore, a lot of the snook on the flats have been caught three or four times, so they know what it means when they see a fisherman and they haul tail. You have to be cautious or you won't catch many, even though there may be lots of fish available," says Hawkins.

There are a number of ways to reach out and touch fish before they know you have nefarious designs on them. First is to use a rod and reel that can throw a reasonably long line, yet is not so cumbersome as to be hard to handle. Obviously, the distance champion is the "Hatteras Heaver" type surf rod, but these giant 12-footers are impossible for use in the confines of a flats boat, and very tiring for repeated casting. However, a stiff, two-handed graphite baitcaster or spinning rod in the 7-foot range can throw a lot of line--enough to catch fish even in the exceptionally clear waters of early spring, before the algae bloom puts color in the water.

Fill Your Spool

For distance casting, it's particularly important to keep spinning reel spools filled all the way to the lip of the reel, even though this will mean occasional tangles as too much line shoots off the spool. In fact, a spool filled to within 1/8 inch or less of the rim is probably the single most important factor in adding distance with a spinning reel. You have to pay more attention to the reel to prevent extra loops from creating a mess, but you can gain a great deal of distance by keeping the spool completely full. And the lighter the line, the further you can cast. On identical tackle, throwing the same lure with the same effort, a cast with soft 6-pound test will go 10 to 20 feet further than one with 10-pound test, because there's less drag and less wind resistance in the thinner line. You can even see a slight difference in different brands of the same test. In general, those that are thin and limp give the best distance, but in spinning line, a bit of

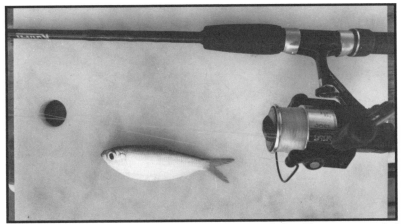

Fishing live sardines often requires reaching distant potholes. The narrow-spooled "long cast" reels like this one from Daiwa provide extra distance without casting so hard that the bait is flipped off or killed.

"spring" seems to make the line jump off the spool more easily and helps distance a bit. Monos with a shiny finish may cast just a bit further than dull ones, too, because of drag over the lip of the reel and through the guides, but some anglers think the shine is obvious to the fish on bright days, so avoid it.

Tackle Care

Proper tackle care can help distance, too. The free-spool on baitcasters has pretty much done away with gear drag problems of years gone by, but for smoothness of operation and dependability after the strike, baitcasters need to be taken completely apart at least once a year, cleaned in solvent, have worn parts replaced (pawls and drag washers are likely candidates in snook reels) and then be reassembled with proper lubricants added to the moving parts. This needs to be done even if the outside of the reel looks like new. The combination of salt and old oil makes up a hidden sludge inside the cover and in the level wind gears that greatly cut the smoothness of the reel. (Don't overdo it with oil, though, and make sure to use a very light grade on spool spindles to allow free rotation. Too much just makes a mess, and excess can drip on your line, causing a scent trail that the fish won't like.)

If you're using an older spinning reel, take a close look at the lip of the spool for the white residue that sometimes builds up there, a combination of salt and monofilament dust. This needs to be rubbed away with very fine steel wool, or with rubbing compound, because it creates a noticeable drag on the line. While you're at it, you may want to give the lip of the spool a rub with a hard-finish auto wax, which makes it extra slippery and, again, cuts down on drag.

With older rods, you naturally want to make sure all guides are in excellent shape, not grooved from long use, and with no cracked ceramics or frames that are bent out of line. Two-hand rods will allow you to throw much farther than one-handers, because you can use a pivoting action, pushing with the reel hand while you pull with the butt hand, to greatly increase rod speed and power. Most anglers find a handle about 12 inches long, from the butt to the center of the reel seat, provides good leverage for tossing most inshore plugs, yet is not so long that it's tough to "walk the dog" or perform other maneuvers with the rod.

Gaining Distance

Learning to get lots of speed into the rod and letting go at the right moment for maximum distance is a matter of experience. But anybody can learn to add a few feet to their casts by what they do with the rod while the lure is in flight. On the upward arc, the rod should be pointed upward, following the flow of the line after the lure. As it begins to fall, however, if you tip the rod down, following the drop of the lure so that the line does not have to flow off the tip top at a sharp angle, you'll gain several extra feet just from that slight reduction in drag. A lot of anglers finish their cast where they end the power stroke, at about 10 o'clock, but they're robbing themselves of maximum distance by doing so.

You can also use the wind to your advantage to gain extra distance. If you want to fish a light, wind-resistant lure like a Rapala or the DOA plastic shrimp, you can make long casts with it by fishing downwind, and throwing the lure high into the air, so that the wind "kites" it out toward your target. This is less effective with dense lures like jigs, but there's some increase in distance with them, as well.

Among the tricks for gaining distance to reach snook like this one, which was working near the distant shore, is to keep the reel filled to capacity, and to follow the flow of the line with the rod tip.

If you have to fish upwind, however, it's best to put the wind-catching lures away and go with dense, compact lures like spoons and jigs. A sidearm cast, hard and fast and as close to the surface as your skill will allow, will give the best distance because it scoots along under the wind.

The average angler will get better distance either upwind or down with spinning gear, though the real pros can throw more line with a baitcaster because the revolving spool sort of "shoots" line off after the lure, rather than requiring that it be pulled off as in spinning. Fishing upwind with a baitcaster is tough for most anglers, because backlashes are an endless problem when you're trying to punch the lure out there a few extra feet.

Of course, if you plan your approach to a fishing area right, you can often have the wind in your favor. This can add many feet to your casting distance, and allow you to stay further from the suspected snook lair, thus probably improving your chances for a hook-up.

For example, if you're working a pothole on an outside flat, it will often pay you to make a large circle around the spot, staying at least 150 yards off, to get in a position so that the wind pushes the boat toward the spot. This allows you to shut down the outboard, and you don't even need to handle the pole or the trolling motor, either of which usually creates some noise as you're getting ready to put them into operation. The wind will sail you right to the spot, if you give it an assist with the outboard skeg.

You do this by simply steering as you would if the motor were running. The stern will always hang into the wind because of the drag of the prop in the water, and if you turn the wheel left, the lower unit acts as a rudder to sail the boat left. You can maneuver considerable distances to either side in this way, making your approach completely silent.

You do want to have the anchor ready, however, because if you don't, the wind will keep right on pushing you until you're too close to the hole, blowing the fish out. The idea is to have the anchor sitting on deck, preferably on a towel to muffle noise, with the line untangled. When you get to the point where you think you're maybe 20 feet beyond your longest cast to the near side of the hole, ease the anchor over the stern and release 20 feet of line before cleating it off. (You don't need more scope than this because of the minimal depth on the flats. You do need a good anchor, though. A Danforth, sized appropriately to the weight of your boat and with at least six feet of heavy chain in front of the rode, will do the job every time.)

With the wind at your back, you can now sieve the near side of the hole repeatedly to try to stir up a fish. If you have no luck, ease

These long-cast reels all add from 10 to 15 feet to casting range. From the top, they are the Abu Garcia Cardinal UltraCast 64, the Shimano Aero GT-X 8-12A, and the Daiwa PS-1305. More effective than special spool designs, however, is using lighter line and keeping the spool filled.

out another 10 feet of anchor line and do it again. Gradually, you work over the entire spot without ever letting the alleged snook know you're there. You'd have to get a lot closer if you made the approach into the wind, and you'd have to use your trolling motor or push pole to do it. While that works many times, it can be a problem when the water is clear and the fish are nervous.

You can use the tide to slide you into range of distant fish, as well. Current flow works on a boat the same way that wind does, and you can again control the drift by using the lower unit as a rudder, as you approach with the flow.

You can also use a strong current to take your lure to the fish in distant and difficult spots--overhanging mangroves along an under-cut bank, for example.

There are a number of great spots in the Fakka Union River, near Port of the Islands, where just this sort of approach is very useful for getting at snook without getting close enough to spook them.

If you anchor your boat above an undercut bank on the falling tide, you can then cast a floating plug just short of the target, and then allow the current to float it right in under the limbs. When it's in the right spot, you take up slack and begin to dance it across the flow. A pal and I caught 11 good fish on a single tide in the Fakka Union a few years back using this method, all within a hundred yard stretch of shoreline.

New Longcast Tackle

There's some new spinning gear currently on the market aimed especially at increasing casting distance with light lures of the sorts preferred by inshore anglers. Daiwa's "LongCast" models sort of got the ball rolling a year or so back with the introduction of reels with a narrow but long spool. The narrower diameter cuts friction, but the long spool still holds plenty of line for long-running fish.

Shimano is in the game as well with a whole line of "Aero" maximum distance spinning reels and matching rods. The reels also feature the narrow spool design, plus a worm gear that causes variable oscillation in the bail speed, wrapping in a pattern that prevents line from digging into the layer below it. In conventional reels this can be a problem, and any time the line slips between underlying layers, it acts as a brake on the lure in the next cast. Shimano says the reels cut friction at the lip through the narrower spool, and also cut down on the big loop and the centrifugal force tending to throw line outward, rather than straight ahead through the line guides on the rod. The new long-casting rods, the "Aero-Rods", feature guides with extra long frames to hold the line away from the rod. Shimano engineers discovered that line slapping on the blank is the major cause of friction once the line leaves the reel, so they designed the new rods to eliminate the problem. Interestingly, the line guides are exceptionally small for a spinning rod, aimed at reducing the loops of line coming off the reel to minimal diameter immediately, so that they don't touch the rod shaft. This is the opposite of conventional wisdom about spinning rod guides, where it has generally been assumed that larger guides would create less drag. But the system works. Most anglers find their distance goes up 10 to 15 feet with many lures.

Abu-Garcia and other makers now are offering narrow-spool spinners of similar design, with similar gains in casting distance.

Of course, all the fancy gear in the world won't do you much good if you don't learn to see the fish at long ranges, and don't use a lot of patience and caution in the approach. But these days, if you don't fine tune your inshore gear to fish fine and far away, you're not playing with a full deck.

CHAPTER 8

SNOOK ON THE BEACH

SNOOK COUNTRY.

Images of dark water, mangrove islands and grassy bays, oyster bars and creek mouths. Right?

Not necessarily. In summer, think beach blanket bingo. Think surf boards. Think sand.

Snook are most often thought of as fish of the back country, and most of the time that's accurate. But for a lengthy period each year, lots of them, including some of the biggest of the clan, roam the beaches of both coasts of Florida. Anytime from April through October, and later at the southern extremes, big, sea-bright linesiders comb the surf both day and night, looking for mullet, crabs, whitebait, silver trout or whatever else comes along.

And though back country snook are getting enough pressure so that they know the difference between a Maverick and a Hewes these days, those fish in the surf rarely see an angler's hook. They're tough to get to from a boat, because the hump that builds on the outer bar can make things uncomfortable within casting distance of shore, even when the sea is nearly flat calm. That fact alone shuts out 90 percent of the angling pressure from snook addicts, who love their shallow-draft, go-fast hulls. But for folks who don't mind taking off their shoes and stepping into that warm sighing surf (I don't mind if I do), there's a world of angling action.

Some of the best beach snooking in the state has developed over the last five years along the barrier islands from Longboat Key southward to Naples. As the snook population has grown, thanks to

71

tight MFC harvest regulation, fish have become more and more abundant along the beaches--the classic spread of fish range and numbers in a variety of areas indicative of a healthy, burgeoning population.

Most folks are familiar with the typical summer snook jam that takes place as breeding fish crowd into well-known gathering areas like Big Marco, Redfish, Captiva, Stump and other west coast passes. A similar aggregation takes place on the east coast, a bit later, from Sebastian Inlet southward. These aggregations, in fact, are the reason that the snook season is closed from June through August-- biologists figured out that the fish were just too easy to catch then, with the lion's share of the annual harvest coming in only a few months as anglers swarmed over the schools. But because summer harvest has been shut down for years now, those unmolested fish have increased in numbers to the point that they not only provide astonishing catch-and-release action in the passes themselves (Cortez guide Scott Moore and party released 119 in a single day a few years back) but also swell outside the channels and along the beaches, both before and after spawning surges which usually take place on the new and full moons.

The fish are in the surf for one reason, to find food. So they're less likely to be so temperamental and maddening as snook can sometimes be when they're hanging under a dock or sleeping in the mangroves.

They feed most actively, in my experience, on rising water. As you'd expect, the rise brings crabs and sand fleas out of their holes, and puts lots of small fish up high on the beach, where they're easily pinned by a rushing linesider. Rising water at dusk, dawn, or after dark is particularly good, especially if the annual shoreward migration of blue crabs coincides--as it does through much of the summer.

Locating Beach Snook

Snook might be anywhere along a beach, but numbers are usually highest within about 400 yards of a pass. You'll also be likely to find fish around sandbars that shoot out from the beach, like those around Cayo Costa and Don Pedro islands near Fort Myers. And particularly good are areas where rock groins have been set along

Though most go to the beach for sun and surf and sailing, snook anglers know that big linesiders often prowl close to the sand. Fishing along the beaches is particularly good in mid to late summer, as mature fish finish spawning and go on the hunt for food.

the beach to prevent erosion. Snook seem to hang around these areas on both low and high water.

When seas are calm, as they often are in summer, you can sometimes actually see snook in the surf, cruising the swash channel between the beach and the bar or finning along just under the surface. As when sight fishing on the flats, you need the sun behind you, and a pair of Polarized glasses to cut the surface glare.

Where you see one snook along the beach, there are usually more--the fish tend to roam in loosely scattered schools that may spread out over a couple hundred yards of beach, where ever there's a bar or rock pile for them to center in on.

Short Casts for Long Fish

The neat thing about these surf fish is that you don't need a 12-foot "Hatteras Heaver" to reach them. Your standard backcountry snook gear will do just fine--a medium-weight popping rod, a level wind baitcaster and a spool full of 12- to 15-pound test mono is just right, as is a 7-foot, two-handed spinning rig with 8 to 10 pound test. The fish are likely to be close to the beach, so the larger tackle necessary for surf fishing for blues or other species often found well outside the surf is not needed. If you can cast 125 feet, that's usually all you need. And many times you'll see fish close enough to touch with the rod tip.

In fact, probably the reason most initiates don't do all that well on the beach is that they fish behind the fish. The snook are likely to be within 20 to 50 feet of the beach, the area where the breaking waves keep the water stirred into a slight murk and where they can better ambush baitfish tossed around in the undertow. The guy who makes 300-foot casts out beyond the bar is not going to be showing his lure to many snook, though he might hook some Spanish mackerel or maybe a tarpon.

I've seen snook charge right into the shallows to pick off baitfish, churning along with their backs half out of water as they blasted through the minnows. The fish are usually looking toward the beach, or at least parallel to it, rather than out toward the open water. Snook also eat a lot more crabs than most folks suspect--check a snook stomach next time you clean one and you'll almost surely find some shell remnants. The crabs are frequently found right in the spin-drift where sand meets sea, another attractant that keeps snook looking "uphill".

Lures For The Surf

Topwaters are the most interesting baits to fish in the surf, though by no means the only lures that work. Traditional killers like the Zara Spook, the Bomber Long A and the Cisco Kid get plenty of ferocious strikes when darted along through the waves, and smaller lures like the Bangolure SP-5 or the 5M or 7M Mirrolure will also do the job. Generally, silver or white finishes get the nod, though some anglers now swear by the new purple series of MirrOlures.

The Zara seems to work best when fished with the classic "Florida whip" that makes the lure hunt back and forth with each twitch of the rod as the reel is cranked rapidly. It's exhausting fishing, but good for some monster linesiders. Another lure that works much like the Zara, but with less effort on the angler's part, is the Bill Norman Rat'Lur. The other lures mentioned above also catch fish when worked fast, but they do just as well when worked in a series of short, sharp jerks, with brief pauses between--and this sort of action is much less tiring to the average fisherman.

Sinking plugs are also effective in the surf, with the 52M MirrOlure and the Bagley Finger Mullet two of the favorites. The lures are fished within a couple feet of the surface, in a series of short hops. A well-known bass lure now becoming a hot item for snook in the surf is the Rat-L-Trap, a vibrating lure that looks very much like a sardine. The 'Trap is cranked fast and steady.

Jigs also do plenty of business along the beach. White or metal flake versions are good where there are lots of glass minnows or small silver baitfish, while dark brown or root beer is favored if the snook appear to be feeding on crabs or shrimp. The lures should be allowed to tick bottom after each hop, but the hops should be short ones. Some folks insist it's necessary to fish a hundred miles an hour to draw a hit from a snook, but most of the time you'll catch more at moderate speeds--and your arms will last longer, too.

Casting Patterns

Whatever the lure, the casting pattern should begin parallel to the sand, falling in water just deep enough to float a fish--maybe a foot. Make the retrieve right down the beach line. If that doesn't get a hit, drop the next one about 4 feet further out and try again, and so on until you've fanned the area all the way out to the "green bar", the sandbar that causes a green strip of water to appear at the edge of the beach slough along much of the Florida coast. If you don't score, walk down the beach to the point where your first cast landed and repeat the pattern.

And when you stick a fish, come right back to the spot where you got the strike when the battle ends. Often, whatever held that first fish there will attract others, and you may hook a half dozen more without ever moving. Or, you might not. That's snook fishing.

Prospecting the beaches by boat makes it easy to hit a lot of likely looking spots in a short period, and when the waves are minimal it's no problem to pull up within 50 feet of shore, anchor the boat bow

Lunker snook are probably more abundant along the beaches than in the more "classic" snook country of the mangroves and oyster bars. Fish in the 20-pound class are rare in the backcountry, but raise few eyebrows along the beaches, either on Florida's East Coast, or along the Caribbean Coast of Costa Rica, where this fish was taken.

to the seas and wade ashore. If the surf is over a couple of feet, though, you'll probably find it too difficult to use the boat, unless you can run inside an inlet to anchor and go ashore, then walk back around on the beach to fish.

In fact, the inlets often offer some of the better fishing opportunities when you're waiting for the tide to start rising along the beaches. As the tide falls out of the sounds and bays, it pulls tons of baitfish, crabs and shrimp through these passes, and snook are usually in a feeding mood when all those groceries start passing overhead. You can fish the fall at the pass, then walk out along the beach as the tide starts to return. (When fishing the outflow, work it like a trout stream, casting up-current and bouncing the bait as it comes back down with the tide.)

The Mullet Run

The fall mullet run along East Coast beaches is the ultimate opportunity for catching a lunker snook anywhere in U.S. waters. Experts like Capt. Mike Holliday of Stuart routinely catch at least one 20-pounder daily when the run is on, usually beginning the last week of September or the first of October, and peaking by Halloween.

The technique is to find the mullet schools, cast net a bucketful, and then run out an eight-incher on a 6/0 hook, right back into the school. The monster snook are never far from the bait, and when the dinner bell rings, they rush the mullet, creating a "shower" of leaping fish. The one with the hook in it is a bit slower than the rest, and gets gobbled. It's almost a lead-pipe cinch for a trophy.

The beach may not be "classic" snook country, but when you hook a seabright giant, you'll forget all about mangroves and black water for a while.

CHAPTER 9

HEAD THEM OFF AT THE PASSES

IN THE GOOD OLD days of snook fishing, some 70 percent of the annual catch came from the passes during the spring and summer spawn, beginning around the full moon in May on the west coast and extending through the end of August on the east coast. In those days, up until the mid-1970's when DNR biologist Jerry Bruger figured out that too many snook were being killed by fishing during the spawn, anglers from all over the country gathered in spots like Big Marco Pass and Redfish Pass, both in southwest Florida, in such numbers that the fleet of boats was similar to that swarming over the tarpon at Boca Grande. It was a great fishery, but like so many great fisheries unregulated, it invited overfishing.

With the closure of the spawning period a decade ago, most of this pressure disappeared. The prime spots in the prime times these days rarely attract a half-dozen boats. But for anglers who don't mind catch-and-release snooking, a visit to the passes in spring can provide some of the best action and biggest fish of the year.

Where To Find Spring Spawners

Among the most productive passes, on the west coast, are Stump, Gasparilla, Captiva, Redfish and Big Maco. On the east coast, inlets from Sebastian southward all have snook pods in spring and summer.

Snook not only stack into the major passes during this time, but also school heavily in much smaller flowages, anywhere that strong

Whether you fish from shore or from a boat, fishing the passes during the summer spawn is one of the most productive of all techniques for fast action and big fish. At one time, up to 70 percent of the annual harvest came from these passes in summer, but current regulations allow only catch-and-release fishing.

tides will sweep the eggs into large bodies of water. The eggs need to be supported by strong flows for 18 to 36 hours to hatch, and these conditions are found in many of the larger bays on the west coast. Snook sometimes gather around the channels between small bayous and larger bays in remarkable numbers. The Port Manatee channel, in Tampa Bay, is locally famous for producing huge numbers of big fish. There are also good numbers at many of the small but deep channels leading from the estuarine bays into the larger harbors along the west coast, including the Joe Bay, Bishop's Harbor and Cockroach Bay channels on middle Tampa Bay, and the deeper cuts between most of the islands outside the Skyway Bridge on the south shore of lower Tampa Bay. Also good are the areas where causeways span this bay, creating stronger current flows.

Charlotte Harbor has spawning aggregations at the mouths of Bull and Turtle Bay, as well as in the deeper passes between islands in Pine Island Sound.

And on the East Coast, the fish often move out along the beaches adjacent to the inlets to drop their eggs.

Wherever you pursue them, the techniques for catching spawners are much the same.

Scot Brantley shows typical bright, stout summer spawner from Captiva Pass. The fish was taken by free-lining a live sardine after skipper Larry Mendez had chummed a school of visible fish into a feeding frenzy.

Pass Fishing Techniques

The classic method is to float a live pinfish through the deepest sections of the pass, keeping the bait just off bottom and just clear of the rocks that usually litter the spots where the snook gather. This is usually an outgoing tide fishery, with boats drifting along directly above their baits to avoid snagging. You add just enough weight to the line to keep the pinfish straight down beside the boat. A good LCD sonar will actually show you the schools of fish, so you know when you're about to get a bite.

In some areas, such as Redfish Pass, this type of fishing is so well established that anybody who tries to fish otherwise, by anchoring, is likely to get some hard advice from local guides who don't like amateurs fouling up their act. It really does work better to keep drifting, and one anchored boat in the midst of a drifting fleet is trouble for everybody, so it's best to follow local custom.

You can also fish live mullet this way, and many on the East Coast prefer this bait, in lengths from six to 10 inches. A big mullet is safe from the sailcats that also prowl the passes, and is especially attractive to monster snook, in excess of 25 pounds, that are sometimes encountered in these waters. (These giants don't very often show up in the backcountry. Evidently they move back out into the open sea after the spawn. An interesting question for speculation is whether or not there are as yet undiscovered aggregations of these giants somewhere far offshore, like the adult redfish of the Gulf of Mexico, or whether snook just don't, on average, survive to weigh much more than 25 pounds, with the occasional 30 to 50 pound fish an aberration, like the 7-foot-tall human.)

When the snook pod up in somewhat shallower water, as they frequently do, the schools can be spotted by smart skippers who make use of a spotting tower and Polarized glasses. The fish will often mill along the edge of a pass, in water six to 10 feet deep, and when the water is clear, they can be seen at these depths. Sometimes you can see individual fish, but more often it's just a changing mass of darker green than the surrounding water.

When the fish are spotted, the skipper drops anchor at the edge of casting range, and chums the spot with live sardines, much like the

82

Capt. Scott Moore of Boca Grande was one of the originators of the live sardine technique for fishing the passes. Moore's methods have allowed him to catch and release up to a hundred snook in a single day at times.

backcountry snook guide. Once the first few fish pop at the baitfish, it's all over--the entire school will have food on the brain, and when the sardine with a hook in it arrives, it lasts less than five seconds.

This is the sort of action that allows top guides such as Scott Moore to produce catches of 50 and more fish per trip. It can be absolutely gangbusters, with frequent doubles and even triples if you have several anglers aboard.

Oddly enough, though, when the snook are hitting the sardines, they won't even look at the most careful presentation of an artificial. Once, fishing with Moore, I worked through every known snook lure, often running the plugs right next to his live sardines, and while snook were falling all over themselves to eat the livies, I got never a look on any fake. (If somebody figures out what it is that allows snook to make the distinction, they'll have a killer lure. Maybe the baits put out a distinctive smell, or vibration--whatever, when a snook is looking at a live sardine, he won't touch plastic, wood or feathers most of the time.)

There are plenty of times when pass snook will take artificials, however. Plugs and jigs are particularly effective on strong outgoing tides early and late in the day and after dark.

A 52-M MirrOlure or a Bagley Finger Mullet drifted with the tide is a deadly offering in spots like the north bar at St. Lucy Inlet or the bars at Captiva and Stump pass. The lures are fished like trout flies being presented in a stream, cast well up-tide and then allowed to come down with the flow, with slight twitches of the rod to activate them as they drift. When the lure stops, you set the hook.

You can also do some good with deep running lures and jigs in the deeper passes in daytime, if you fish them much like the guides fish live pinfish. The idea is to keep the lure almost straight down beside the boat by dropping it rapidly in water 15 to 25 feet deep, jigging it vertically for a few strokes, and then retrieving when it starts to balloon out behind the boat. When tides are running strong (and when fishing is best) you only get a minute of bottom time with each drop, so you have to work at it, but it can be effective.

The idea of the vertical jigging is that it keeps the lure from snagging the rockpiles that are a part of the bottom of most productive passes. With the lure hopping straight up and down, it's much less likely to catch Mother Earth than if you pull it sideways along bottom. The fish frequently congregate around the snaggiest parts of a pass, too, so you need to try to deal with it.

You need a stout line, naturally, 20-pound-test or better, both to control the fish as you go shooting through the pass and so that you can pull free from the less-insistent snags. A stiff rod is needed, too, to set the hook against the arc of line that develops in the current.

Some of the better lures for this work are the 65-M MirrOlure and Cotee plastic-tailed jigs in weights from 3/8 to 1 ounce. The idea is to select a lure that's just heavy enough to hit bottom as you drift, but no more. Too much weight makes snags more likely, and doesn't draw as many hits as a lure that sinks a bit slower.

Moon Phases

Biologists running plankton nets around spawning passes have noted a definite increase in the number of snook eggs released in the three days on either side of the new and full moons. It may be that the strong tides then are best for suspending the eggs until they can hatch, but whatever the purpose, this tells the angler that the time to seek snook in the passes is on the stronger moon phases. (You'll catch fish at other times, too, but if you can plan only one trip per month, it makes sense to make it when everything is in your favor.) Probably the best single fishing period in most spawning months is the night of the full moon--the day of the full moon is also good, but not quite as strong as the night.

Ethics Of Fishing The Spawn

Snook survive catch-and-release fishing well, provided they're handled little and released promptly. And there's no question that snook numbers have climbed steadily since the spawning season harvest was brought to an end, despite considerable release-fishing activity. So, given the present conditions, it looks like conservation conscious anglers can enjoy release fishing during the spawn without concern that they're upsetting the reproduction process in any important way, even though some individual fish caught and released may lose some or all of their eggs for that season. A single successful female puts out hundreds of thousands of eggs, so there should be no shortage of young, even given the high natural mortality of the sea, if the present laws remain in place.

CHAPTER 10

TOPWATER SNOOKERY

THERE ARE EASIER ways to catch snook, it's true.

But snook and topwater plugs were made for each other.

There's absolutely nothing in all of fishing that compares with the maniacal fury of a linesider gone bonkers over a schlurping, dancing floater.

Part of it is the unexpected violence, sort of like getting blind-sided by an NFL fullback. One moment, there appears to be no snook within a mangrove mile. The next--BLAM! SPLAT! ZONK!-- holy sardines, Batman, you're attached to a homicidal piscavore whose only mission in life is to fold, spindle and mutilate your plug and the rest of your tackle around the nearest oyster bar.

The sound a snook makes when savaging a topwater is heard differently by different anglers, just as the citizens of different nations have different descriptions of the rooster's crow. For some, it's a CHUG! For others, BALLOOEY! Some favor POW!

The only universal is the exclamation point after.

Whatever, it's fast and hard, and as exciting when a fish misses as when they connect. Sometimes, more so. I once had a 10-pound fish come up on a Bangolure six times in a single cast, getting more frantic to kill the pesky minnow with each strike. On the last attack, about five feet from the boat, he caught the lure sideways in his jaws and crushed it right in half. The hooks on the front end held him long enough to give us both some exercise.

To be sure, the topwater is not a lure for all seasons. There are times, in the dead of winter, when a slow-moving jig creeping near bottom in a deep hole is a lot more likely snook offering. Neither is the floater the all-time most productive of snook catchers. Live sardines will almost always outfish any topwater (or other artificial) by a considerable margin. So will shrimp, sometimes.

But during the temperate months, when many linesiders spend most of their time in what we lovingly know as the "backcountry", they are poignantly subject to the wiles of topwaters. A surface lure cast next to a mangrove shore, against an oyster bar, or over a hole in the grass flats, you might say, sings a siren song to summer snook. (If you can say sings a siren song to summer snook.)

During this same time, they readily hit floaters along the beaches and in the passes, provided you fish those areas at times when the fish look shoreward for food. Every now and then, you can even lure a big pass fish to the top in 20 feet of water or so, with a big, noisy plug like the Zara Spook.

The Best Lures

Speaking of which, the Zara is probably the all-time favorite topwater for snook. In the hands of a man who knows how to "walk-the-dog", it is an awesome tool. The Zara has no action of its own, but when you work it right, it advances across the surface in a darting, zig-zagging motion that provokes incredible strikes, sometimes bringing fish completely out of the water in a somersault.

The trick, with the Zara and similar stick baits, including the Rat'Lur and the 95M MirrOlure, is to get the lure started with a slight twitch of the rod to the right, slack briefly to allow it to slow momentarily, and then bring it back with a sharp twitch left, followed by another moment of slacking, then the right twitch, slack, left twitch and so on. The reel is used only to take up slack line, not to move the plug. Some guys get good enough at it that they can keep the lure jumping back and forth even though they twitch only to the right or only to the left, which is less tiring, like paddling a canoe on the same side instead of switching. (After an hour of jerking a Spook, you'll think you ARE paddling a canoe if your wrists are not in shape.)

There are two problems with the Zara, though. One is that, if the fish are not in an aggressive mood, they won't chase down this noisy, fast-moving plug. The other is that, unless you've got wrists like a

Topwater plugs are both deadly and exciting. And, in some waters, they're the only way to get at the fish. Any lure which imitates a silvery baitfish can be effective. Shown here is an SP-5 Bangolure.

gorilla, you get tired of working it pretty quickly. In the right place, though, it can be one of the best, particularly for big fish in somewhat deeper water where they might not see a less obnoxious plug.

One of my personal favorites, though, is the Bangolure SP5. This is a lipped plug with a tail spinner. It weighs about half what the Zara does and consequently won't cast as far, but it's far easier to work, it's effective at lower speeds, and snook love it. (So do trout and reds, for that matter.)

With the Bango, the most effective action is less vigorous than that with the Spook, though somewhat similar. The idea is to send it twitching just under the surface, then slack the line briefly so that it pops back to the top. Each time you snatch it under, the tail spinner sends out a little "burp" of water. The lure often turns sideways when you slack the line for that instant, so that when you pull next time it darts and flashes, and this action seems to drive snook nuts. (Bangos work a little better if you remove the snap ring on the hook eye, and instead tie your leader to the eyelet directly, with a loop knot to allow free movement.)

The floating Rat-L-Trap is a strong snook lure, too, probably because it so closely resembles a sardine. This can be worked in a series of rapid cranks or jerks, or simply cranked straight in fast enough to make it vibrate and rattle. Either way, it's a killer.

MirrOlure makes a number of superior floaters. The 5M is particularly good, but most anglers like to unscrew the eye and remove the front spinner before using this lure. The front spinner is not needed to produce adequate noise, but it tends to twist the leader around itself, fouling the plug frequently. With the front spinner gone, the plug sits a little higher in front, too, which seems to make it work better.

The 7M MirrOlure is also a great snook plug, as is the smaller version, the 38M. Neither of these have any action of their own, and must be worked with the rod tip like the Zara. The 38, in particular, looks remarkably like a wounded sardine when you get it working just right. With a little practice you can learn to make this little lure actually jump out of the water, as a fleeing bait sometimes does, and snook can't stand it. The trick is give a short, sharp upward flick of the rod tip when the lure has turned sideways. It splashes and skips with a remarkably lifelike motion. (Don't think the little lure won't attract big fish, either. It's the plug that light-tackle master David Fairbanks of Largo used to set all four of his line-class world records.)

There are times when snook are very nervous--in clear, shallow water on a calm day--when you need a lure that makes very little disturbance. The Number 11 Rapala is a good choice for those days. It's too light to make long casts on anything other than light spinning gear, and the hooks are too small to hold a big snook if you use heavy line, but it will draw strikes when others fail. It's fished like the Bangolure, in a series of short, sharp twitches that make it dive, then spring back to the top. For snook, you don't need to hesitate more than a half second after each jerk--you don't want to let it set until the ripples die, as largemouth bass fishermen often do. A snook usually loses interest in any artificial that sits still for more than a few instants.

The Bomber Long A, the Cisco Kid, Goldeneye and similar large, lipped floaters can either be worked as jerk baits, or can be cranked steadily to draw hits. Some anglers like to reel the Bomber just fast enough to make it wobble along at the surface, an effective winter trick around powerplant outflows. And some like to "burn" a Cisco Kid, cranking it as fast as they can reel. When a snook takes hold, you know it.

It's sometimes necessary to pole your way into waters too shallow even to operate a trolling motor. In areas this shallow, the topwater is one of the few plugs that will function. In general, the shallower and calmer the water, the less action expert anglers give the plug. (Courtesy Outboard Marine Corporation.)

Color is probably not very important in topwaters, since all the fish can see very well is the bottom. But most experts generally choose silver, white or chrome finishes to resemble baitfish, usually with blue or green backs. Some guys like black or dark purple after dark, on the theory that it offers a sharper silhouette against the sky. And I've even caught fish on glowing pink floaters. Choose colors that make you happy--you'll be looking at them a lot.

It's interesting to note that not all "identical" lures are identical. Due to small variations in manufacturing, some model D58 Flopdoodles just work better than all the others of the same model, and some Flopdoodles don't work well at all, even though they appear to be alike in every detail. Anglers who luck into a "perfect" plug treasure it for years, guard it with their lives, and will go to any lengths to rescue it from snags above or below water.

After you gain some experience with topwaters of a particular model, you can tell in one cast whether you've got a good one or an also-ran. The best ones seem to have a special dart and flash, brought out by the slightest twitch of the rod. They don't hang their hooks on each other, and they don't snag your leader with their prop.

Some guys go to great lengths to sort the wheat from the chaff, buying up to a dozen identical lures at a time, then taking them home for a quick test in the swimming pool. The ones that are winners go into the tacklebox, and the others go back for a refund.

Sometimes you can turn an average lure into a great one with just a bit of fine-tuning, however. If you have one plug you particularly like, compare it closely to one that looks the same but doesn't work the same. Sometimes the hook eye on one is just slightly off center, or twisted. Or maybe the prop has a bit more pitch, or less. In wood plugs, there might be variation in the buoyancy, based on different lots of wood--maybe you can add a bit of lead foil to a lure that's too light, or put lighter hooks on one that's too heavy. Sometimes the screw eyes are turned in close to the body, sometimes they're left out a turn or two--and it can make a difference.

The snook may not be as particular as the snookers, but the idea is to fish a lure you have confidence in. That can make a big difference, even if the precise action of the lure doesn't.

Topwater Techniques

A lot of anglers get discouraged with floaters because they get lots of strikes, but few hook-ups. If you find they're not getting stuck, it usually means either that the plug is too big, or that you're moving it too fast. (A question for speculation: how can a snook bite a lure with nine hooks and not get stuck? Especially when those same nine hooks will reach out and grab anything else--mangroves, oysters, the upholstery of your car--that comes within three feet?)

When a fish strikes and misses, you can often get him to come back by letting the plug stay where it landed, and just wiggling the rod tip enough to make it bob up and down in that spot. If you don't get an immediate strike, give it one quick twitch, then wiggle it again. Usually when the fish doesn't get hold, he stays close, watching to see what his potential dinner will do. If it looks too vigorous, the fish figures there's no point in extending the energy to try to catch it

A stout graphite baitcasting rod like this one is needed to work a topwater effectively, and to set the hook promptly when a strike comes. Experts caution against setting too soon, however--the plug is often taken away from eager fish before they get a firm grip.

Some have trouble knowing when to set the hook, too. Getting it right requires watching the plug itself, not the splash the fish makes. A lot of times a tremendous, splashy strike does not take the plug down, while a quick little "chug" does. If you're not looking at the lure, you can't tell if the fish has got it. And if you set when he's not there, your lure comes jumping back into the boat at you, instead of staying out there where the fish can come back and connect.

Tackle For Topwater

It takes a stout rod to properly control a floater, but the stick, and the reel, should be very light in weight. A two-handed graphite popping rod, with very little hardware in the reel seat, is the ticket. Your reel should weigh no more than 10 ounces, because it will feel like 10 pounds by the time you make 400 casts with a topwater. Best is a light baitcaster of the sort used for largemouth bass--you don't need 200 yards of line to land a snook in the mangroves.

On the other hand, you do need fairly stout line, which lets most spinning tackle out. Snook seem to understand that there's safety in cover, and that's where they go when they feel the hook. If you're fishing 6 or 8-pound test, you can forget trying to stop them. And using line much heavier than that on a light spinner leads to casting problems, so a good free-spool baitcaster is the best snooking tool. The minimum line test is 12, which gives best casting, but you'll land more fish with 15 or 17 or 20.

Remember, though, that even with this heavier stuff, you don't lock down the drag as you might to deck a "hawg" bass. Set the drag at about 1/3 the test of the line, so that the fish can't get a solid pull against it--a 10-pound snook can break 20 like sewing thread on a direct straight-away run, and even if the line doesn't break, the hooks on most plugs will straighten under that kind of stress. You want the drag to give you a safety margin. You can apply more drag with your thumb, as the fish charges for the mangroves, right up to the limits of the line test.

One area where spinning rigs do work, and in fact are superior to baitcasters, is on the grass flats, where it takes long casts and thin lines to even get a strike, and where there's lots of open water to fight the fish. In these waters, you can whale out a small, lifelike lure with one of the new long-cast spinners to reach fish that would be untouchable with a baitcaster. The light stuff provides great sport, too, in these areas where mangrove roots are usually not a problem.

The same conditions apply along the beach, though there, if you're without a boat, you'll occasionally lose a fish that simply heads for the horizon, if you depend on 8-pound to stop him.

Best Lines And Leaders

I avoid fluorescent lines for topwaters. They are much too easy for a fish to see. Clear lines are best in most waters, but in blackwater rivers many experts switch to black mono. Snook can be very temperamental at times, and you're better off taking away as many of the negatives that might put them off as possible.

There are two schools of thought on shock leaders for floaters. Once says keep it as short as possible, so that it doesn't interfere with lure action and is less obvious to the fish. These guys (I'm included) use an 18-incher. Others prefer a longer leader, on the theory that a long leader gets the knot well away from the plug where the snook is less likely to notice it. And the longer leader gives better protection from the sharp gill covers when a big fish sucks the plug well down. With an 18-inch leader, he may cut the line when he turns, while he'll only fray a 24-inch leader.

Long or short, use fairly light shock for floaters, no more than 25 pound test, to keep the visibility minimal and the lure action at a peak. As always, use no snaps or swivels. Attach the plug with a MirrOlure loop knot to allow it to work freely.

Keep Your Plugs Perky

Floating plugs require a bit of maintenance to remain effective. If the hooks get bent, as they often will after a few big fish, it's best to replace them with new ones. Deformed hooks affect the action of many topwaters. Be sure to use exactly the same size and wire diameter on the new hooks as on the originals, or you may ruin the action as well.

Also, make sure the line eyelet does not get bent or turned sideways, because this too can turn a great plug into a mediocre one. And on wood plugs, look out for cracks and pinholes in the finish. Once water penetrates the wood, the plug will become heavy and lose it's quick, darting action. You can sometimes bring an injured plug back by allowing it to sun-dry for several days to get all the moisture out, then sealing the finish with a few dabs of polyurethane varnish.

View any repaired plugs with a jaundiced eye, however. Sometimes, very subtle changes are enough to change the action just a bit, and that may turn off the appetite of a temperamental snook.

CHAPTER 11

THE FALL MIGRATION

SNOOK ARE AT the northern limits of their tropical range in Florida, and thus have to make special accommodation when the water cools below 70 degrees. The fall migration into coastal rivers is evidently caused by this need to seek deeper, and therefore warmer, waters, without leaving the rich feeding areas of the estuaries. It's possible that a considerable number of snook also move offshore, to deepwater reefs, but there has been very little documentation on this sort of migration thus far.

The movement away from the flats, beaches and mangrove backcountry takes place in late November and early December most years, with the arrival of the first big cold fronts of the year. The wind, rain and plummeting temperatures of the fronts quickly chill the yard-deep flats where snook summer, and start them pushing for more comfortable territory.

The migration is gradual most years, with the fish moving into the river mouths and lower ends of inside passes, deep creeks and manmade channels with the first fronts, and then progressing landward with following storms. When there are warming trends after the first front or two, a fair number of fish move back out on the flats, sometimes traveling several miles from the refuge of the rivers.

By Christmas, however, you can depend on there being snook far up most coastal rivers. Fresh water does not stop this migration-- snook survive very well in water that supports bass and bluegills, and the latter is a frequent food of winter fish. I once put four 20-inchers in a half-acre freshwater pond near my Hillsborough County home,

With the first cool weather of fall, snook begin to move toward coastal rivers and off the shallow flats where they feed in summer. By late fall, bass anglers well upstream in flowages like the Peace and Caloosahatchee often catch both largemouth and snook on the same lures.

and those fish survived there for three years, reaching weights of close to 10 pounds (on an all-bluegill diet) before a major January freeze killed them. Further, considerable numbers of snook migrate all the way to Lake Okeechobee up the St. Lucy and Caloosahatchee waterways, and enough of them get through the locks to produce a pretty decent fishery at times around the rocky areas on the southeast shore. In the Everglades, migrating snook run all the way back into alligator country, providing good fishing in creeks so narrow that a boat can barely turn around.

Finding Fall Fish

The trick is to find how far along the migration has moved. There's no point in fishing the headwaters of coastal rivers in early November, because nearly all the fish will be to seaward. On the other hand, if you fish the lower end of a river during late December and early January in a cool year, you're going to be fishing below most of the fish.

The best way to get on the fish is to put the trolling motor on high and start pitching a topwater to the shoreline, working upstream as fast as you can cast and crank. The idea, at this stage, is just to draw a hit or make a fish show itself, rather than to catch anything. You'll pass by quite a few fish working this fast, but until you draw a hit, you

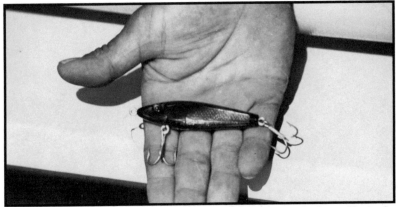

Small, dark plugs like the 38M MirrOlure in the "purple demon" shade are effective for fishing the rivers in fall. Many anglers bend down the barbs on these lures, so that they penetrate more easily on light lines. The crushed barb also makes it easier to release snook unharmed.

don't know if you're fishing in the right ballpark, so it's necessary to move rapidly.

A second alternative, in water that's not too narrow and convoluted, is to troll until you connect. Snook readily take trolled lures, and a 52-M Mirr-O-Lure or a half-ounce Rat-L-Trap pulled along steadily covers a lot of water in a short time. Shallow-running wobblers like the Bomber Long A, the Rebel, the Rapala and the Bangolure also do the job.

Or, you can drift with the current, and trail live baits behind the boat on floats. The same golden shiners preferred by largemouth bass are taken eagerly by snook. So are small bluegills and tilapia. The baits are suspended about four feet below the float, with enough weight to keep them down there instead of ballooning up behind the float. If the current is moderate and there aren't too many snags, you can also simply free-line the live baits. Either way, if they pass through a pod of migrating fish, things will happen in a hurry.

Once you establish that you're in snook territory, you can switch to conventional winter techniques to catch them. That means slowly twitching a floater along the shorelines for the smaller but more abundant fish to five pounds or so, or anchoring and putting out large live baits in the deep bends and holes for lunkers.

Snook become particularly active during the occasional Indian summer periods when afternoon sun warms the shallows. They'll readily hit fast-moving topwaters at such times, though they prefer slower-moving offerings when the water is cool.

If you seek fall snook in a powerplant outfall, you can make use of a surface temperature gauge to outline the perimeter that will be likely to hold fish. The heated water from a generator creates a plume that may extend a mile or more from the plant, with this water at 70 or above while the surrounding bays are in the low 60's. A temperature gauge makes a very noticeable leap when you enter the warm water. You don't need the gauge on a cold, still morning, because the heated water will create a wall of steam where it begins.

If there are flats within the warm water area, you may find snook in this zone during the early part of the fall migration. They're particularly likely to hang around rocky rip-rap areas and channel edges in such entry areas. When it gets really cold, though, most of the fish will huddle right up at the sluice gate where the hot water comes out, and you need to get as close to that area as you can to score.

CHAPTER 12

WINTER SNOOKING

SNOOK ARE FISH of summer, as everybody knows.

Snooking time is skeeters and no-see-ums and afternoon thunderstorms. Snooking time is sunburns and 92 in the shade. It's top waters and cold beer, mangroves and oyster bars, secret spots with special pals.

Except that snook don't necessarily understand all of that.

And so a lot of them keep on feeding, right through the dead of winter. And they do it in some very unsnooklike spots.

When the gray wall of December's first big front comes blowing in, the snook have to get off the flats and out of the shallow salt creeks where they've spent the summer. If they don't, and if the water drops much below 70, they'll get stiff as the proverbial molasses in January. If water temperature drops below 60, they'll die.

So the fish are on the move in winter, looking for what might be called "snook spas"; warm water refuges to escape the cold.

There are several possibilities. The most obvious is to migrate offshore to the reefs of the Atlantic or the Gulf, and there's growing evidence that a lot of linesiders do just that. A number of divers have reported seeing masses of snook over offshore ledges and wrecks in recent years.

But until somebody figures how to locate them with some consistency, these offshore fish are of little interest to anglers.

Much more intriguing are the large numbers of snook that move inshore, into coastal rivers, canals, ship channels and turning basins.

Snook are thought of as shorts and sneakers summer fish by many, but they continue biting well even when anglers must wear hats and jackets. In extreme cold, though, it's necessary to find the temperature refuges where fish gather to avoid cold shock.

These fish gather in generally known areas that are easy to reach by small boat, or even from shore in many cases.

The fish seem driven to push as far upstream as they can manage, almost like salmon seeking a spawning rudd, though the linesiders won't spawn until they return to the bays and outside passes in late spring and summer.

Where to Find Winter Fish

Thus, some of the tiny creeks of the upper Everglades offer gangbuster snooking in mid-winter, back in those narrow little spots

A small boat and portable outboard are often the ticket for pushing far back into brackish water creeks in search of winter snook. Some of the best action of the year is available in Everglades creeks in December and January. (Courtesy Outboard Marine Corporation.)

where the spider webs drape over your face as you round each bend and you're as likely to catch a largemouth as a linesider on every cast.

The same is true of the many rivers along the west coast, where waters like the Caloosahatchee, the Peace, the Myakka, the Manatee, the Braden, the Little Manatee, the Alafia, the Palm and the Hillsborough all attract winter fish, the latter three despite rather serious pollution problems.

Despite their relatively northern location, there's also good snooking, in the Anclote and the Pithlachascotee, at New Port Richey. This is about the northern limit of the species on the west coast except for splinter populations in the spring-fed waters of the Homosassa and Crystal rivers.

On the east coast, all the short rivers and canals in the Miami to Palm Beach area hold winter snook, and they run far up both forks of the St. Lucie River. In fact, some fish go all the way to Lake Okeechobee, through the locks and into the lake, where they occasionally astonish winter bass anglers along the east shore. The canals at Vero Beach hold some good fish at times in winter, but any further north the numbers are spotty. Some big fish are caught now and then in the canals as far north as Port Canaveral and Daytona Beach, but it's not dependable enough to go looking for them.

All of the larger rivers in Everglades National Park and in the Glades west to Naples hold winter snook in considerable numbers, but as indicated earlier, you often have to get a long way back in to find them. Take a chart and keep a close eye on every bend, or you may spend more time in there than you want to.

Again like salmon, snook tend to migrate inland until something stops them, such as a dam. They'll stack up below such structures, especially if there's lots of water coming through, and such spots are always good for a fish or two after frontal rains get things flowing.

Other prime locations for winter snook are the proliferating electrical power plants along our coastlines. Though some of these are noted polluters of both air and water, there's no question that the hot water outflow from the generator coolers acts as a magnet for snook in cold weather. Some of the larger plants, such as the giant TECO facility on the east shore of Tampa Bay, put out a plume of 70-degree water that reaches over a mile from the outlet, creating a broad refuge for linesiders at times when they'd be numbed by cold otherwise. Similar facilities at Fort Myers, Port Everglades and a number of other spots around the state are also dependable snook producers in January and February.

Techniques For Winter Snooking

Winter snook can dependably be caught on jumbo shrimp, pinfish and other live baits, but a lot of sportsmen try to avoid using the natural baits during the closed season in January and February when the fish must be released. They reason that the naturals are usually taken deeper in the throat, and thus result in more mortality of hooked fish. Artificials usually get no further than the jaws, thus make it easy to remove the hooks without permanent injury.

If you fish at anytime other than the January/February closed season and want to make use of the live baits, however, they'll do the job. Because the fish are somewhat slowed down in many winter locations, the slow action of a large, live shrimp seems particularly

A small jig eased along bottom is one of the best offerings for snook during cold weather. Large, heavy jigs work in deeper water, but sometimes they appear to be too big for the reduced appetites of winter fish.

attractive to them. The crustaceans are best fished on an un-weighted 2/0 hook, with the requisite 18-inch piece of 30-pound-test mono shock leader to prevent cut-offs on the gill plates. The standard hook-up, just under the horn on the shrimp's head, works as good as any. A medium spinning rig with 10-pound-test will do the job unless you fish in areas with close cover, such as the mangrove creeks. There, you have to use something that can handle 20-pound test line, because every fish will head for the roots when it feels the hook.

Best way to fish the shrimp is simply to pitch it into areas where you expect fish to be, such as the deep channel bends of a coastal river, or next to blowdowns extending over deep water, or around docks and piers, and let it drift and swim along where ever its whims and the tides take it. You'll catch a lot of reds and trout in some areas in winter this way, too, because they like the same sort of refuges the snook do--and you'll also get a surprising number of largemouth bass in some areas where the water is fresh enough--bass like the shrimp taste, too.

When it comes to artificials, plastic-tailed swimmer type jigs like the Cotee shad are hard to beat. The gold fleck model is especially effective in stained water like that in most west coast rivers. It doesn't take a big jig to catch a big fish, either. I caught a 20-pounder on New Year's Day a few years back using a 1/8 ounce head, the size most anglers use for fresh water panfish.

When it's really cold, the fish seem to hold close to the bottom, so you fish the jig down there in a series of slow hops, feeling it up and down with a taut line. At the slightest bump, you set the hook. (In power-plant-heated water, though, remember that the fish may be active on the coldest day. That Jan. 1 fish hit right on top as I was reeling in, and put up a tremendous battle on 8-pound gear, showing summer energy because he was only a hundred yards from the outflow in steaming, 75 degree water.)

You can also do very well on powerplant fish on topwater lures, though these work better after dark when the other anglers have gone home and the fish prowl the top, looking for bait stunned in the turbines. Bangolures with the tail spinner, the SP-5, are a good choice when worked in a series of short jerks--not the rapid, dancing retrieve of summer. A steadily-cranked wobbler like the Cisco Kid will also do the job, as will the 52 M MirrOlure, a slow-sinker, or the 7M, a floater.

You can also do well at powerplants by fishing the outflows with shrimp imitations such as the DOA, a remarkably life-like plastic molding that's weighted to travel upright through the water, just like the real thing. The hooks are buried inside the lure, with the line connection also within. You tie on by threading the line through the lure to the removable hooks, then pulling them back into position.

With this lure, you anchor as near the outflow as allowed (most rope off the first 50 to 100 feet due to turbulent water) and pitch the lure into the boil, allowing it to drift rapidly back with the current. You don't have to give it much action, just take up the slack. Remember, a live shrimp doesn't swim very fast except when it's frightened-- normally, it just sort of eases along with it's little swimmer feet twitching, barely faster than the tide, and that's how you want the DOA to behave, as well. If it stops, you set the hook.

Occasionally, you can also draw fish by skittering the DOA, giving a sharp pull to make it flip up on top before returning to a slower retrieve. This works well around lights after dark, where the fish may be looking toward the surface for shrimp.

Sometimes the fish are in the flow itself, sometimes in the eddies along the edges. They also stack up at times at the first shoal downcurrent from the outflow.

Small jigs that look like shrimp also work in this situation. In general, the smoke or rootbeer colors that are similar to the natural brown of the shrimp work best. In shallow water, you may need to go with a small head weighing no more than a quarter-ounce, but with a larger tail than normal to add buoyancy.

Topwaters sometimes work in the canals and upper rivers, too. The Rapala is a favorite along the west coast. The same sizes used for bass, the R-9 and R-11, get plenty of hits when dapped along shoreline on light gear. The light hooks will straighten if you fish them on heavy line and heavy drag, however, and if you put heavier hooks on, they ruin the action. Fished on light spinning gear and 8-pound-test, they draw lots of strikes, and if you're lucky, you'll land plenty of fish.

Crankbaits also work well at times. The new saltwater version of the Rat-L-Trap, in chrome, is a favorite on the Pithlachascotee River and some others. A steady retrieve around bridges and piers does the job. The lure also works well when fished around areas where marsh creeks dump into the main river channel--concentrate on these spots on falling tides.

Winter fishing hangs on most years until near the end of March, with the fish gradually staging down the rivers and creeks and sometimes gathering in considerable numbers around canal and river mouths in early April before heading into the bays and passes to spawn in May. That's when the traditional snooking crowd comes out to meet them, but for those who'd rather not wait, there's plenty of linesider action available all winter long.

CHAPTER 13

FLY-RODDING FOR
FLORIDA SNOOK

SNOOK ARE GENERALLY thought of as a species that prefers a large, noisy artificial or an equally large live bait, but in the right waters, they're also suckers for a well-placed streamer fly or a fly-rod popper. In fact, a decade ago biologists from the Florida Game and Fresh Water Fish Commission involved in a zero budget snook propagation program found the most efficient way to catch the numbers of spawning snook they needed was with a streamer fly twitched along the bottom of the coastal passes after dark.

The fish that are easiest to catch on fly tackle are those found in the clear, shallow flats that stretch out around the Intercoastal Waterway between St. Petersburg and Naples--about 200 miles as the crow flies, but with lots of extra water added in by sprawling Tampa Bay and Charlotte Harbor.

Snook are often thought of as fish of deep passes and murky-water mangrove country, but in this part of the state they regularly prowl the clear grass flats, resting in sand-bottomed holes where the water is no deeper than four feet.

Fishermen who know where to look and what to look for have learned to sight-fish these snook--some of which weigh in excess of 20 pounds, and most of which are willing to attempt eating fly-rod offerings.

Fishing is usually best in areas where lots of tidal flow crosses a flat, bringing with it plenty of sardines, shrimp and small crabs. Points around mangrove islands are also productive.

Fishing these areas at maximum tide flows, guides like Ray DeMarco of Anna Maria Island and Paul Hawkins of St. Petersburg regularly put their clients on lots of fish over the 24-inch minimum size limit.

Fly Tackle For Snook

Because of the shallow, clear water, it's necessary to be able to throw a long line to catch these fish consistently--casts of 60 to 80 feet are often needed to prevent spooking the fish. A size 9 rod with a 10 weight forward floating line (WF10F) is a good rig--the slightly heavier line makes it easier to cast without getting a lot of line out through the guides. The floating line would be preferred for flats and mangrove country, while if you try them in the passes in spring, you'd go to a sinking tip. Mount a light reel with a smooth drag, with capacity to carry several hundred feet of backing in case you stick a bruiser. (You don't need one of the custom-made $350 machined aluminum models for snook, though. Scientific Anglers makes some nice ones for a whole lot less, as do some others.) The leader can be standard saltwater issue, starting with a butt of 30 pound test about three feet long, followed with another three feet of 20, then the required 12 inches of line-class tippet, then back up to a foot of 30 for shock leader. The butt is tied to the fly line with a Nail Knot, while the other connections are Blood Knots or Surgeon's Knots.

Chum Them Into Range

If your saltwater fly casting skills are a bit rusty, you may have to be smart instead of good. Bring along a live well full of Spanish sardines, and use them as chum to lure the snook into your casting range. (If you fish with a guide, let him know in advance about your casting range, and he'll make sure the live well is loaded.)

Just about any dark-colored streamer tied on a 1/0 heavy wire hook will do the job on snook--stay away from bulky flies, though, because they're hard to throw long distances. A fly that looks something like a sardine is good, if you find one that doesn't have a lot of fluff tied in. The good ones breath out when you hesitate, but are very streamlined when in motion.

Snook readily hit flyrod streamers in passes during spawning period. They also smack poppers presented along mangrove shorelines, and the flyrod is a particularly effective tool for working the strike zone in such cover.

Other Flies

In poppers, chartreuse, white or green heads with matching feathers do the job. Neutral buoyancy flies are also good. They're tied with just enough bucktail or other flotation to keep them drifting along a foot or so under the surface.

In the shallowest areas you'll do best if you wade, because this keeps your profile low--you're less likely to spook the fish. And wading is also the coolest way to fish during the prime snook months, from April through October. If you go from June 1 through August 31, it's catch and release only, of course.

Working The Fly

Snook are by far easiest to catch at the peak of tide flows, and the fly needs to be presented moving with the flow. It's something like stream fishing for trout. You make the pitch up current, bringing it back just fast enough to keep out slack and make the fly jump

Snook can really strut their stuff on fly tackle, because there are no treble hooks or heavy jigs to impede them. The small hooks are easy to remove without injuring fish, too.

forward in six-inch hops. The slow-sinkers are best in this situation, and the line should be a floater to allow for ease of casting and pick-up.

The flyrod is a uniquely efficient tool for working a mangrove shoreline, because it makes repeated delivery to the strike zone very quick and accurate. If you keep the boat at the right range, every flick of the rod puts the bait back against the roots. Strip it four or five times and then lift and deliver to the next crevice in the bank--it's a deadly way to fish when the water is up in the roots.

The trick in landing snook on the fly, as in catching tarpon, is to "clear" the loose line after the strike. There's usually a tangle of loose strippings on the deck when the hit comes, and as soon as the hook is set, you have to concentrate on getting that up and through the guides smoothly before you do anything else. Once the fish is on the reel, it's the usual test between your skills and the tippet to keep the fish out of the snags, and the long rod and light fly give the snook an unusual opportunity to strut his stuff.

Fish don't often take the fly deeply, and even when they do, it's a simple matter to snake a Hook-Out or long-nosed pliers down the leader, get hold of the fly and back it out in most cases. You never get the damage that a treble-hooked lure sometimes does, which means it's more likely that the fish can be released successfully to fight again.

You can make it even more certain by bending down the barbs on your streamers and poppers, or filing them off altogether. De-barbed hooks don't seem to come loose during a fight any more often than those with the barbs, but they're a lot easier to get out after the battle.

In fact, the barbless hooks may have a slight advantage in landing fish, particularly with fly tackle, because the long, flexible rods don't put a great deal of pressure on the hook at the set. There's some evidence that the de-barbed hook goes home easier because there's less resistance. The barb is the major deterrent to getting a hook buried in the jaw of a fish, the largest diameter that has to be forced into the flesh. With the de-barbed hook, it's as though you're using a super-sharp hook of exceptionally fine diameter, yet you have the strength of the heavier hook material in the shank and bend.

The single hook of the fly also makes it easy to land snook without use of a net, since you can use the same lip-lock as that used in bass fishing. You don't want to try this when there's a treble-hooked plug in the fish's jaw, but it's safe with the single fly. (If you lift a snook larger than five pounds via the jaw grip, be sure to support the body with your other hand, applied around the anal fin. Lifting big fish by the jaw alone is likely to dislocate the jaw, or strain the backbone and neck, and though the fish may swim off after release, it's not likely to survive long term. For those you plan to take home to dinner, this doesn't matter, of course, but for anything beyond the limit, it does.)

CHAPTER 14

NIGHTSTALKERS

SKEETERS BUZZ. Gators bellow. Bull bats roar. Nighttime in mangrove country is not peaceful. Not for the creatures under the water, either. Because snook are nightstalkers.

They feed far more actively after the sun goes down, and for those willing to brave the bug bites, the unseen snags and the invisible backlashes, night snooking can be incredibly productive.

Not only are the fish more naturally inclined to feed after dark, but also the low visibility makes it tough for cautious fish to spot boats and fishermen. And there are no jet skis zipping over the heads of the linesiders every 10 minutes, no other fishermen offering them a tackle shop full of lures. For the artificial lure tosser, the reduced visibility makes it far more likely that a fish will mistake plastic and feathers for the real thing.

Mangrove Country After Dark

Fishing mangrove country after sundown is the most challenging of night-time snooking, but can also be the most productive. You'll be faced with absolutely incredible hordes of mosquitoes, especially when your lure lands in a mangrove, which it often will, and you go in close to retrieve it. You may go aground on unseen sandbars, and you'll almost certainly get backlashes that you can't see to untangle. If all of this sounds like your idea of fun, you might make a backcountry nightstalker.

117

The fish are active in the same places and under the same conditions as during the day, so the way to be successful after dark is to have a complete daytime knowledge of the area you want to fish. This means knowing exactly where the shallow flats, oysters and sandbars are, so that you can stay clear of them in your boat. Don't guess--run compass courses and times in tricky water, so that you can be sure you won't spend the night aground. You'll be amazed at how easy it is to get temporarily disoriented (some people call it "lost") when you get into the backcountry after dark.

A LORAN set on your backcountry skiff can be a great help in after-dark navigation, keeping you precisely informed of your position anytime you're uncertain, and helping you sort out that one pass where you expect the fish to be from all the look-alikes out there in the gloom.

In general, you'll find the fish around the points, up on the bars and against the trees on rising water, and at the creek mouths, passes and points on the fall.

If you fish areas where grass flats meet mangroves, you'll find active snook in the potholes on the flats during low water, though you may have to wade to get to them without making them nervous. (True, wading after dark may make YOU nervous, but, hey, part of this fishing stuff is to prove you're a macho guy, right? Just remember, everything out there is more scared of you than you are of them. You hope. Sharks are not so much of a danger as they were before the days of the long line, but sting rays are abundant and active at night. Move slowly and shuffle your feet, and try not to whimper when you step on a flounder.)

Piers and Bridges

By day, monster snook love to sleep under public fishing piers, hanging there like big green logs, as if they were paid commercial advertisements for the pier operator. They never bite, just hang there, making angler's mouths water.

But they have to eat sometime, (don't they?) and that sometime is usually shortly after the sun goes down. The lights go on then, at piers and at many highway bridges, and these lights have the same influence on shrimp and baitfish that a porch lamp has on bugs. It

118

Fishing after dark can be uncomfortable, but it's usually far more productive than fishing the daylight hours. Snook are naturally nocturnal feeders.

draws them in, dizzied and disoriented, making easy pickings for the predators.

The best bait for these locations is whatever happens to be running through at the time, so it's wise to bring a castnet and collect your bait on the spot--shrimp, Spanish sardines, finger mullet, needlefish--whatever. Some guys, like the late Clyde Parrish of Tampa, like big baits for this night work. Clyde's modus operandi was to jig up a 12-inch ladyfish or trout, then impale the hapless fish on a forged 5/0 and waltz it around the pilings on 100-pound test and an inch-thick Calcutta pole until all hell broke loose.

Or, if you like to keep it simple, you won't go wrong by buying a couple dozen jumbo shrimp. The usual assortment of floating and sinking plugs and jigs are also effective at times, particularly around private docks where the fish don't see so much of a selection.

The fish don't automatically start eating the instant it gets dark, however. They still wait for the tides to make it easy, with the exception of a few eager beavers that will announce themselves with watery explosions as they slam a bait against the pilings. The big feed can come on either the in-flow or the out, and coincides with some

119

regularity with the solunar feeding periods, when these come on tide peaks. (Speaking of which, by far the best tidal chart ever invented is the Tide Rule, devised by Lane Thompson and now marketed by Southern Saltwater. The Rule shows an amazingly simple and accurate representation of exactly when and how strong local tides will be for months in advance. Every snook angler needs the current edition of the Rule in his wallet.)

In murky water, you can often catch night snook directly under your feet. It takes some patience to keep the bait swimming for hours at a time without a strike, but when those guys lying in the "shade" from the lights decide to eat, your bait will be first on the list.

In clear water, you'll see plenty of fish next to the pilings, but it's hard to catch the fish you can see. Better is to fish for those you can't spot, but that will nearly always be lying just at the outer limits of the ring of light. The fish apparently cruise here, where they are invisible to the baits blinded by the lights.

Your bait should work right along the dividing line between light and dark, and on out to 10 feet or so into the dark area. With live baits, just cast up-current and let the critter drift with the tide, retrieving when it completes a sweep. Don't let it hang out there like a kite on a string, because the only thing it will collect that way is weeds--you have to actively cast and retrieve for best action. In general, you won't need any weight on the line--just let the bait swim where it wants to. Sometimes, though, in deep channels or passes, you may need to add a bit of weight to get down where the fish are, but never enough to bounce the offering off bottom.

Sometimes snook stay smart even after dark. There's one particular dock on Gasparilla Island (better known as Boca Grande) where loads of snook gather under the lights every night, but they won't hit anything but the live shrimp that come drifting through every now and then. The only way I've ever found to catch these guys is to literally crawl out on the dock like you're sneaking up on a big whitetail buck, just barely peek over the edge to get them located, and then lower an unweighted jumbo shrimp down to them, to the point where he can just barely swim in a little circle. After he does that for a while, one of them usually can't stand it and POW. You only get one a night of these sophisticated critters, but it works.

Gasparilla is also the site of one of Florida's most famous snook holes, the old phosphate docks on the southeastern tip of the island,

Finding your way after sundown can be a major undertaking. It's particularly easy to get disoriented in mangrove country, where every island looks the same after dark. Some anglers use LORAN to locate their spots and find their way back home. (Courtesy Aquasport)

just inside Boca Grande Pass. The rickety and long-unused docks are an incredible tangle of ancient pilings, cables and junk standing in water as much as 30 feet deep, and it's stiff with some of the biggest fish on the West Coast. Everybody knows it, but not many people ever get one of them out, except for the privileged few who get an invitation from the owners to fish from the dock itself. From the docks, the Calcutta pole is standard tackle, and experts use up to a pound of weight to hold their baits down in the current.

However, it's possible to anchor just off the dock (big anchor and lots of scope are a must) and drift a weighted pinfish or jumbo shrimp back into the danger zone. Falling tide is best, and the fall really rips. It takes some weight to get the bait down to just the right depth, and you can't let it sink all the way to bottom or you're snagged instantly.

It's no picnic to control a 20-pounder once hooked, either, since he's within a few feet of cover and the tide is with him. It takes 40-pound tackle, minimum, to have any hope. Some guys use their 80-pound tarpon gear. And even that gets broken sometimes. It's a different kind of fishing, but interesting to try.

Snook also hit readily along the beaches and passes after dark. With the swimmers and surfers gone, big fish often move to within a few feet of the sand to feed on crabs and mullet.

Artificials are worked the same way, though with them you have to retrieve somewhat faster, thus make more casts. With a sinking lure or jig, you want to just kiss bottom on occasion. Floaters and slow sinkers should be worked just a bit faster than the tide.

Bridge and pier gear has to be on the heavy side to land any fish. The Calcutta pole and 100-pound-test has much to recommend it if you want a trophy, but you can do ok with a standard popping rod and a baitcaster loaded with 30 or 40 pound test. (Don't lock down the drag on your light-weight bass reel against 40, though. It will result in stripped gears or a bent spool, and still no snook. The heavy line, with a medium drag setting, will allow you a lot of control and abrasion resistance, and if you don't pull hard when the fish goes around a piling, you can often get him to swim back out, or perhaps wade in and follow him until things get sorted out. With lighter line, it's over before you can start to negotiate, and the same is true if you try to use brute strength while the line is against a piling. It takes a bit of finesse to know when to back off, but finesse works better than power once the fish is under the cement.)

Beach And Pass Fishing

A lot of snook prowl the surf and the main passes after dark, often entering knee-deep water where they're never seen during the day. For really big fish, 20 pounds and up, there's no better opportunity than working these areas. And the fish are there to feed, so they readily take an assortment of artificials, including streamer flies.

The beaches are usually most productive on the rise, as the fish move into the slough between the first bar and the beach. Fish right along that bar and in the slough, casting parallel to the beach as you wade along where the waves break.

The passes are best on the fall, as countless shrimp, crabs and baitfish are sucked out to sea. The snook stack up to feed on them. You simply pitch your lure as far upcurrent as you can manage, and bring it back down, twitching occasionally until it stops in a fish's mouth.

Since fish in these areas tend to run big, and since the waters are usually easiest to fish from shore, it makes sense to use large-capacity reels for fishing beaches and passes. Either baitcaster or spinner should hold at least 250 yards of 10-pound or better. A really big one will occasionally swim straight offshore with all of that, but most swim more or less parallel to the shore, and you can control them by following.

This fishing remains good from the start of the spawn on into October and maybe November in warm years. The only thing that puts it off is big winds, which muddy the water and make it hard for the fish to see the lures.

Let There Be Lights

Where ever you fish night snook, you're going to need light. On bridges and piers, it often pays to carry a gasoline or propane lantern, and hang it down next to the water to attract bait--and snook--right under your feet. If you fish from a boat, you can do likewise, or use a 12-volt floating lamp of the sort freshwater crappie anglers use, operated off the boat battery.

You also need a light to see to tie on lures and pick out backlashes. Most guys get along with a flashlight held in their mouths when needed, but you'll do a lot better with some sort of headlamp. The best I've seen is a tiny high-intensity bulb on a flexible neck that mounts on a baseball cap and operates from two AA batteries set in the sweatband. The thing weighs only ounces, lasts a full night on one set of batteries, and puts the light exactly where you need it. It's sold under the trade name "Speedlight" at many tackle stores.

Bugs

You will also need several large, industrial strength drums of insect repellent, if you fish snook country after dark anywhere other than on a windswept ocean beach. Mosquitoes and no-see-ums are just as active as snook during the night, and they will just about fly away with you in some remote mangrove areas. If you've never been introduced to Everglades mosquitoes, it can be a frightening experience to hear the entire swamp begin to roar as the sun sinks. It's audible a long way from the trees as literally billions of the little blood-suckers take wing.

For this duty, you not only need a high-DEET repellent, you also need a long-sleeved shirt, thick socks, pants, and a broad-rimmed hat with a headnet. It's hot and uncomfortable, but essential on a windless night if you hope to stand it. (Forget "natural" repellents or electronic bug repellers. Mangrove bugs laugh at them.)

No-see-ums are not much bothered by DEET, but don't like whatever it is they put in Avon Skin-So-Soft lotion. The stuff is remarkably effective in tests where anglers have doped one side with the rosebud-smelling lotion and left the other eau-de-sweaty-fisherman. So, you need a bottle of the stuff, in addition to mosquito repellent, especially for those dawn and dusk periods when the unseen little monsters are most active.

Night fishing is not easy and some guys say it's not even fun, but no body argues that it's not productive. If you can put up with the difficulties, you'll catch more snook than you'd dream of taking in the day.

CHAPTER 15

SNOOK BOATS

UNTIL VERY RECENTLY, a snook boat could be anything from a 12-foot rowboat to a 25-foot cabin cruiser. There were no fishing machines designed specifically for the pursuit of snook, in the way that the bass boat is designed to chase bass. That's slowly changing these days, with more and more hull designs targeted for the inshore flats angler. Some of them may look a bit strange, but there's no question that they're deadly when it comes to getting to those hidey holes where the lunkers have been able to grow unmolested by deep draft boats of years gone by.

The basic parameters for a good snook rig include a very shallow draft, no more than a foot at rest and preferably less. This means it must have a flat or modest vee bottom, plus some way to get cooling water up to the outboard when it's trimmed to the max, pretty much level with the bottom of the boat. Some accomplish it with stern pockets, like those used on the Hydra-Sports 1750 or the Action Craft. Others opt for tunnel construction, like that on the Shoalwater and some of the Texas flats barges. Lengths range from 16 to 20 feet, beams 7 to 8 feet.

The ultimate rig needs to be fast, capable of running in the 40's or better, to make those long runs from Flamingo to the outback at Shark River and beyond, and with adequate freeboard and forward flare to keep waves out of the cockpit when crossing open bays. It needs storage for at least 10 rods, considering all the extras snookers love to carry, with both horizontal racks to store spares and verticals to store "working" rods. It should have plenty of unobstructed deck area both fore and aft, so that anglers have lots of room to swing a rod. It does not necessarily have to be "poleable", as a bonefish or tarpon skiff does. For the most part, snook water does not demand poling, and snook don't appear, yet, to be so sensitive to the whir of the electric positioning motor as are bones and silver kings.

If you fish live baits at all (and most snook anglers will learn the art, sooner or later) it should have a killer bait well, large and deep, with rounded corners so the sardines or mullet don't stack up and die. The well should have a minimum of pipes and fittings down inside, because baits will find a way to get stuck behind them. And it should have a large, easily removable stainless wire screen to keep scales from jamming the pump. The pump should be a high-capacity marinized job that will shoot a steady stream of new water all day long, but without eating up your battery completely. There should be an overboard drain for excess water, another overboard drain for when you want to drain the well at the end of the day.

Bonefish boats and even aluminum jon boats 15 to 16 feet long make great snook boats, especially if you fish alone or with only one partner. They're light, fast, and run in extremely shallow water on minimal power. If you run aground, you simply hop out and push off. If you fish a couple of buddies, you'll want a larger hull, 18 feet or maybe more. These require more power, but better carry the extra weight of more anglers and gear, plus the heavy live well for live bait angling. If you run aground, however, you wait for the next rising tide.

Among manufacturers currently building boats of interest to snook anglers are Action-Craft, Bay Hawk, Hewes, Hoog, Hydra-Sports, Lake-and-Bay, Mako, Maverick, Renegade, Shoalwater and Silver King. Conventional freshwater bass boats are also excellent for chasing snook in protected waters, as are flat-bottomed, aluminum jon boats.

Trolling Motors

Most anglers have discovered by now that the electric trolling motor is an essential part of a snook rig, and those mounted on the bow serve most types of fishing a lot better than the stern mount variety. You'll probably want a 24-volter, and be sure to select a motor designed for saltwater, with corrosion-proof metals. There

Snook boats must be shallow-draft, and light enough to be positioned easily with an electric trolling motor. The Hydra-Sports 1800 (now designated the 1750) is a useful snook rig in most waters. It features a stern "pocket" that feeds water to the prop, allowing it to run in just 12 inches of water, plus a bow deck for a trolling motor.

are a lot out there directed at the freshwater bass market, and they don't last a year on the coast. I personally like foot control models, but many prefer a manual steering version to eliminate the tangle of cables on the deck. Those who have towers on their boats (see below) may like the versatility of the electrical steering models like those from Minn Kota and MotorGuide, which allow the use of a pair of foot plates, one in the bow and one on the tower, so that you can steer from where ever you happen to be.

In terms of power, the more, the better. You'll frequently be working against wind and tide, and the relatively heavy saltwater boats require plenty of push to get them moving, even in calm water. Opt for a 12/24 volter, because the 24's burn less current per pound of thrust. Most anglers find they need at least 40 pounds of thrust for the typical 17-foot center console. Get the extra long shaft models, 42, 48 or 50 inches, because you'll frequently operate in choppy water, and a short shaft pulls the prop out of the water as you rise on each wave. As this is written, the strongest motor on the market is

Trolling motors, preferably 24-volt models, are essential for silent boat control in the shallows. Be sure to buy only "marinized" motors built with non-corrosive materials that will survive in saltwater. The unit shown here, from MinnKota, has an electric remote steering control that allows operation from the bow or from a tower.

the new 58-pound thrust OMC. OMC trollers score high in corrosion resistance, too, and have long been the quietest on the market.

Outboards And Riggings

Don't underpower your snook boat. It's false economy, because without lots of authority on the transom, your boat will have a poor hole shot no matter what rigging tricks you use. There's no need for overkill, hanging a 150 on an 800-pound hull, but you want adequate push to get you up and moving quickly, even with a couple of buddies and their gear aboard.

The way an outboard is rigged can make or break a snook boat. First, you have to go with a low-end prop, so that you get a very abrupt hole shot. There's no point in running a high-speed prop if you can never get on plane in the areas you fish--opt for a lower pitch and you'll be happier. And of course it has to be stainless steel--aluminum won't last a single day on most flats, where touching bottom now and then is simply a part of getting there. If you have extra change, spend it on a four-blade prop, which provides quicker lift on take-off.

Also if you don't mind spending extra money, a hydraulic jack plate is a nice option to have. This allows you to vertically lift the engine several inches, which is great when you want to idle along in a foot of water, looking for fish. It works a lot better than trimming up, because the thrust remains horizontal and the exhaust stays under water. You can run shallower with the motor jacked up, too. But when you drop it back down, you have plenty of kick for a quick hole shot.

If your boat is slow to plane, you might want to add on one of the oversized cavitation plate boosters, like the Doel-fin. These act as sort of a water ski to plane the stern up out of the water quickly, and also allow the boat to stay on plane at lower speeds. Most who have them like them.

There was considerable interest by shallow-water anglers in jet-drive outboards when Yamaha first introduced them as factory options a few years back, and OMC and Suzuki now offer them as well. But they are not the best choice for fishing the shallow, grassy flats of Florida. The intake is on the bottom of the lower unit, and it tends to suck up weeds on the hole shot, which causes the pump to cavitate. They will run maybe six inches shallower than a prop motor on a flat-bottomed boat, but they burn more fuel, make more noise and provide less speed. They're a must for running the fast, rocky rivers of the Pacific Northwest, but on the grass flats, the conventional outboard is still the best way to go.

Towers

The new half-towers springing from the consoles of inshore boats these days are used not for sighting bluefins or blue marlin, but for the pursuit of snook, reds, trout and tarpon.

They fall somewhere between the towering towers seen on the big offshore boats and the tiny poling platforms dear to the heart of bonefish anglers. But anglers on both ends of the spectrum have long been aware of the fact that "getting high" on anodized marine aluminum gives them a major advantage over their sea-level compadres when it comes to spotting fish.

The mid-sized towers put the skipper's Topsiders 6 1/2 to 7 1/2 feet off the deck, which puts his eyes about 12 feet from the surface. The difference in what you can see from that height and from deck level when crossing a grass flat is the difference between reading in direct sunlight and reading by candle light.

In fact, the tower makes it easy to sight-fish for snook and reds, something not done all that often anywhere outside the clear flats off Flamingo, in south Florida, until recent years.

You can stand up there, easing along on the troller or the outboard, and pick out every fish on the flat if you keep the sun behind you and wear Polaroids. Thirty minutes later, return to the areas where you spooked fish, sneak into casting range on the electric, and wear them out.

The tower is not only a great fishing tool, it's a great help in shallow water navigation, as well. You can see the shallow spots coming a hundred yards away, making it no problem to avoid them, when you're topside. Crabtraps, solitary rocks, whatever, it's easy to avoid the hazards when you have an osprey's view.

The extra height of the tower also turns your little hand-held radio into all but a match for the console models with fixed antenna.

Hydraulic jackplates allow outboards to be raised several inches vertically for the ultimate in shallow water operation. Some boats with jackplate, low water pick-up and a tunnel to feed water to the prop can run in less than a foot of water.

Other pluses of towers in small boats include the additional storage space the tower can provide. It's a simple matter to have the builder add an electronics box right under the tower deck, which is at just the right height when you're at the lower station so that you can reach up and twiddle the buttons of LORAN, depthsounder, or VHF. The location is out of the way, and less subject to water damage than the console itself. And if you want really killer radio reception, you can mount your big antenna up there, greatly extending the range over a gunnel mounting.

131

Specialty boats like the Shoalwater are built particularly for the backcountry. The flat bottom, the tunnel for feeding the prop and the tower for spotting fish are becoming a standard part of the serious snook fisherman's rig.

All of this is not to say that every inshore boat ought to be equipped with a tower, though.

For one thing, unless your boat has adequate beam and weight, the tower is a danger. It acts as a lever on the hull when the skipper climbs topside, and in rough water, that leverage can be enough to actually flop a small boat over on its side. The taller the tower, the more leverage. Any boat with a beam much less than eight feet and a weight under 1200 pounds is doubtful for a tower of any height beyond that of the standard poling platform used in bonefish skiffs. Tower builders work with these problems regularly, and can tell you how much tower, if any, your boat can safely handle. As a rule, flat bottoms and semi-vees can handle more than deep vees, because they're less subject to tipping.

Cost is also a factor--in fact, maybe the major factor for most of us. The materials and the skilled labor needed to make a durable tower don't come cheap. Base for a tower seven feet to the upper deck is around $2,000 or so. But by the time you add an additional hydraulic steering station, ignition switch, padded hip bolsters and electronics box, you may be looking at twice that, and maybe $5,000 or more. That's a mighty healthy bite for most of us, adding as much as 25 percent to the cost of a rig in the 18 to 20 foot range. Tower builders are numerous and all have different prices and somewhat different designs, so it's smart to shop carefully. Where possible, deal with a builder who has made an installation on a boat like yours previously--he may have learned from prior mistakes. And always check with others who own towers by a particular maker if you're not familiar with the make.

Fishing a tower boat takes some getting used to, too, because it puts a major obstruction to casting squarely in the center of the deck. You get used to it, but you always have to be careful with your backcast. And of course, fly fishing would be all but impossible--unless you did it from the tower itself. Talk about lots of space for the backcast!

Some anglers also find that hard-fished species, such as tarpon on the flats, tend to shy away when they spot the approaching tower--and they can see it coming at a considerable distance. Even snook and reds get a bit tower-shy at times, but this occasional clear-water drawback can be avoided by using the boat to find the holes, then slipping over the side to wade into casting range.

Adding a tower to your inshore boat is an expensive undertaking, but for the serious flats fisherman, it's money well spent. Most who have experienced this particular "high" find themselves addicted.

CHAPTER 16

SNOOK BIOLOGY, HABITAT AND MANAGEMENT

COMMON SNOOK BEGIN life about 18 to 36 hours after eggs are released by the females and fertilized by accompanying males in passes leading to large bays or open seas. Spawning occurs from late May into early October, with the peak from June through August. At hatching, they're about 1.5 millimeters long, (.06 of an inch). With tidal help, these tiny wigglers swim inland to the estuary county, where sea grasses, tidal ditches and mangrove roots provide zooplankton food and cover. Within 30 days, they're approaching 1.5 inches in length, and begin to roam a bit looking for larger food, including minute shrimp.

The availability of the estuarine habitat is pivotal to snook survival at this stage. Without adequate seagrass and mangrove nursery areas, the young snook can't survive, creating a "bottleneck" in the life process that limits snook populations, no matter how carefully the mature fish are protected. Thus, most snook biologists believe that the future of snook populations depend on how well the estuaries are protected from development.

One-year-old snook are usually around seven inches long, and they gain another seven inches in their second year. From two to three, the growth slows to levels that will be maintained throughout the life cycle. Recent studies by Ron Taylor and Jim Whittington of the Department of Natural Resources show that fish from Tampa Bay averaged about 19.8 inches in their third year, while those from East Coast inlets averaged 19.3 inches. The scientists determine age by examining the "otoliths" or ear bones of the fish, which show annual growth rings much like trees.

East Versus West

After the third year, East Coast fish generally grow faster than West Coast fish, and appear to live longer, thus reaching larger sizes. Four-year-old males on the West Coast averaged 22.1 inches, while those on the east averaged 25.8 inches. At age five, male snook are about 23.7 inches on the West Coast, 28.2 on the east. Thus, it takes a bit over five years for West Coast male snook to reach the current minimum legal size, while the East Coast fish get there a full year earlier.

Females get larger on both coasts, but those on the East Coast grow more rapidly, as the following table shows:

FEMALE SNOOK LENGTHS, WEST COAST OF FLORIDA							
AGE	3	4	5	6	7	8	9	10
LENGTH	21.7	23.7	26.4	27	29	33.7	35	38.8

FEMALE SNOOK LENGTHS, EAST COAST OF FLORIDA							
AGE	3	4	5	6	7	8	9	10
LENGTH	26.1	28.9	30.7	32.2	33.6	34.8	35.8	37.2

You'll note there appears to be a convergence as the fish approach 10 years of age. That may be because the reduced number of fish that survive beyond age 8 creates a skew in the statistics. Normal mortality these days, results of natural death and hook and line fishing, puts the life span of most snook at no more than 8 years, even though some live longer--and a few live a lot longer, just as some humans live to be more than a hundred, but most die in their

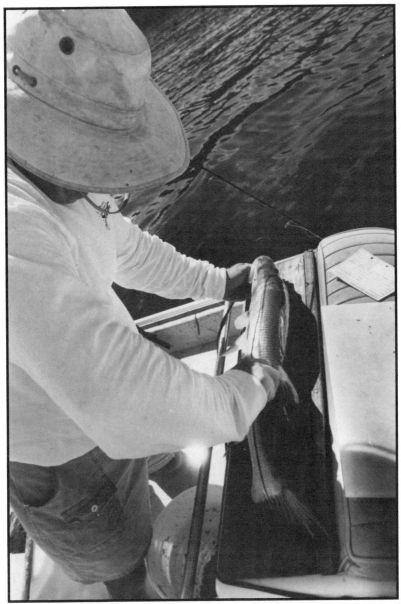

Many anglers tag and measure snook to help the Florida Department of Natural Resources study migrations and growth. This 29-inch fish is probably about 7 years old. East Coast fish were found to grow faster than West Coast fish, at least until age 9.

70's. On the West Coast, few fish in the ninth and tenth year were measured, which may account for their apparently catching up with and surpassing the more numerous fish averaged for the East Coast measurements.

Among the longer-lived fish, a 12-year-old West Coast female taped 38.4 inches. The 12-year-old females captured on the East Coast averaged 37.4 inches. But there were no fish, either male or female, older than 12 years captured on the West Coast. On the east coast, one male was aged at 21 years, a true Methuselah of snook. That fish was only 35 inches long, however. But East Coast females survive into their teens with some regularity, and attain great size when they do.

Fourteen-year-old females averaged 39.5 inches long, 15-year-olds attained about 39.9 inches, and 16-year-olds averaged 41.2 inches. The largest fish recorded in DNR studies came from the East Coast. The fish, aged at 18 years, taped 40.4 inches.

Giant Snook

However, these don't represent the limits of snook lengths. I recently saw a 42-inch fish caught near Port of the Islands. The fish scaled 26 pounds, but was not aged. And the world record snook, caught by Gil Ponzi in Costa Rica in 1978, taped 54 inches and weighed 53 pounds, 10 ounces. Age of that fish is not known, either. A 50-pounder was caught and released at Palm Beach Inlet a few years back according to Ed Irby, formerly DNR biologist for that region and now with the Tallahassee staff.

Even these monsters may not represent the limits of snook growth. There are well-documented reports of fish exceeding 60 and even 70 pounds, and lengths of better than five feet, being sold in Mexican fish markets in recent years. But none of these behemoths have ever been reported to the International Game Fish Association, the record-keeping organization in Ft. Lauderdale, Florida.

The largest fish come from Central America, where there are never cold-kills to wipe out the oldest survivors, and where the always-warm waters produce rapid, year-around growth. Six of the current IGFA records come from the Caribbean shore of Costa Rica, despite the comparatively minimal fishing pressure there, or perhaps because of it.

It takes at least a decade for a snook to reach this size. Virtually all large snook are females, which indicates to some biologists that snook, like grouper, may experience a sex change as they age.

Sex Reversal?

Why are there few males more than 10 years old? Biologist Ron Taylor has an interesting theory. He believes that many males over 500 millimeters long (19.7 inches) undergo a sex reversal. Taylor bases his conclusion on the fact that test nettings turned up a sex ratio of 21.7 females to 1 male for fish over 500 millimeters in Tampa Bay, while the overall average for fish of all sizes was 1.3 females to 1 male. Taylor also collected two snook that were in the midst of the sex reversal process. Sex reversal is common in other saltwater species, and now appears to be the norm for at least a part of the snook population.

Snook Management

The effort to maintain snook numbers despite increasing development and fishing pressure has been a long one, with many reverses as well as some great successes.

The first Florida regulation directed specifically at snook was put in place in 1953 after anglers begin to complain of a notable decline in fish numbers around the southern part of the state. That rule required all fish to be at least 18 inches, fork length, for harvest. It was too little, too late, as heavy commercial net catches combined with excessive takes by hook and liners decimated snook numbers. In 1957, the legislature made it illegal to buy or sell snook, outlawed net fishing, and set a four fish bag limit, with a possession limit of eight.

However, population density studies by Jerry Bruger of the Department of Natural Resources in the late 1970's indicated a 70 percent decline of snook numbers in the Naples area from historic levels, and the legislature moved in 1981 to clamp tighter regulations in place. The bag and possession limit was dropped to two. And in 1982, June and July were closed to all snook harvest to protect the concentrations of spawners in the passes during the time when most of the hook and line catch occurred.

In 1983, the summer closure was extended through 1986, and January and February were also closed through 1986.

This rule was updated in 1985 to make the winter and summer closures permanent, and August was added to the summer closures. The minimum size limit was increased to 24 inches total length, and anglers were allowed to keep only one fish 34 inches or greater in total length daily. These are the rules that are in effect at this writing.

The saltwater fishing license, put in place in 1989, also requires a snook stamp to harvest snook, though the stamp is not needed for catch-and-release fishing. Proceeds from the $2 stamp are now being used to finance snook research that will be used to effectively manage the species into the next century.

Snook Conservation

In addition to the protection of mangroves and seagrasses, snook also need a dependable supply of fresh water entering the estuarine areas to maintain the brackish balance that allows the juveniles to thrive. So protection of water quality in rivers and lakes, development of storm-water retention areas, and prevention of over-use of water for agricultural, mining and residential development are all a part of the concerns of the modern snook angler.

Releasing snook to fight again has been a major factor in the recovery of the species, which has been on the increase since strict management measures went into place in 1985. Snook have not been commercially harvested since 1957.

So is minimization of spraying for insects. It's a given that snook country is mosquito country, and as more and more humans move into the estuarine areas, there are loud calls for control of biting insects. But the sprays used in these control operations are lethal to juvenile shrimp, a major food item for baby snook, as well as potentially damaging to snook eggs. And in higher concentrations, they kill the snook themselves. Spraying needs to be kept to a minimum, particularly during the late summer and fall period when thousands of infant snook are in the backcountry. Unfortunately, this is the same time when mosquitoes are at their worst, and when human residents most insist on spraying.

Efforts at artificially spawning and rearing snook at the DNR hatchery at Port Manatee, on the southeast shore of Tampa Bay, have thus far not met with success, and do not appear to be a likely solution to snook problems in the future. However, there is strong evidence that snook numbers are on the way to recovery due to management measures in many areas, with most East Coast populations holding steady or increasing, and West Coast fisheries producing excellent angling in many areas, though not at quite historic levels. The occasional hard freeze can locally wipe out snook fishing, as it did along the south shore of Tampa Bay in December of 1989 when some 20,000 died, but fish soon repopulate these areas if additional freezes do not follow.

On the West Coast, that repopulation comes mostly from the maturing of newly hatched fish spawned by those that survive the cold. Fish in these waters migrate very little--in fact, there's evidence that those on the south side of Tampa Bay never cross to the north side according to Ed Irby of the DNR. On the Atlantic Coast, on the other hand, fish do migrate considerably, traveling a hundred miles and more from their hatching site.

Self-restraint by anglers is perhaps the best conservation method, putting back the mature spawners and keeping the smaller fish for the table. Snook are not difficult to handle without injuring them or yourself -- they can readily be gripped by the lower lip, just like largemouth bass, in order to boost them into the boat. This is generally better than landing them with a nylon net, which cuts into the slime coat and causes abrasions. Just be sure never to grab a snook under the gill covers, because these are knife-edged and can deliver a severe cut.

To release a fish, set it gently into the water and pump water through the gills by moving it back and forth. After a minute or two, uninjured fish will swim off on their own to fight another day.

Other Snook Species

The common snook, *Centropomis undecimalis*, is by far the most-sought species by anglers, but there are a number of related cousins that produce angling opportunities along the East Coast of Florida, and throughout Central America.

The black snook, *Centropomus nigrescens*, is common on the Pacific Coast from Mexico throughout Central America. It looks much like the common snook, except may be darker in some habitats. It reaches at least 30 inches and perhaps quite a bit more.

The little snook, *Centropomus parallelus*, is found from Palm Beach County southward along the Atlantic Coast of Florida, and is also abundant throughout the Caribbean estuaries. It has a stubby body compared to the streamlined look of *undecimalis*, and is sometimes known as the "fat" snook. It often feeds in large schools at the river mouths. A big one is 24 inches.

The swordspine snook, *Centropomus ensiferus*, is occasionally taken in southeast Florida, mostly by anglers flyrodding for baby tarpon. It's more common in the rivers of Central America. A long, sharp anal spine gives it its name. It rarely reaches 12 inches long.

The tarpon snook, *Centropomus pectinatus*, is occasionally caught in the Everglades area and around the southeast coast of Florida, as well as throughout the Caribbean. The upswept jaw looks a bit like a tarpon. Maximum length is around 15 inches.

CHAPTER 17

SNOOK GUIDES

THERE'S NO QUESTION that getting started in snook fishing is not all that easy. One of the ways to make it easier, and to bring success sooner, is to hire a guide.

Guides in snook country charge anywhere from $200 to $350 per day, usually taking two anglers but some will carry up to four.

If the guide uses live bait such as Spanish sardines, he will net the bait and you won't be charged for it, but the time it takes to catch the bait will be a part of your day. It sometimes takes a couple of hours before you're ready to go, but experience has shown these experts that the bait has to be fresh. Be patient--if the fish are in, the sardines will make you forget the time it took to catch them.

Snook guides also usually have tackle available, though not always. If you want to bring your own, tell the guide what you've got beforehand and he'll tell you whether or not he thinks it's adequate. If you intend to use artificials, be sure to discuss it with the guide, and get his suggestions for the best models.

You should note, too, that most guides these days are strong conservationists, and may not want you to keep fish. It's another point that should be talked over before you book.

If you fish with a guide, you won't need either a saltwater license or a snook stamp, since the guide's licenses will cover you.

Here's a listing of some of the best, at this writing:

Raymond Baird, Jupiter, (407) 746-5266
Phil Chapman, (813) 646-9445
Butch Constable, Jupiter, (407) 747-6665

Capt. Scott Moore is the best-known snook guide on Florida's West Coast. Moore and others have perfected live sardine fishing methods which often produce 20 to 30 snook per day for their clients. Moore is also a noted fighter for snook conservation.

Dennis Dube, Oldsmar, (813) 855-9666
Paul Hawkins, St. Petersburg, (813) 894-7345
Van Hubbard, Boca Grande, (813) 697-6944
Todd Geroy, Naples, (813) 455-7761
Pete Greenan, Sarasota, (813) 923-6095
Bill Miller, Charlotte Harbor, (813) 935-3141
Chris Mitchell, Boca Grande, (813) 964-2887
Scott Moore, Cortez, (813) 778-3005
Phil O'Bannon, Fort Myers, (813) 964-0359
Dan Prickett, Chokoloskee, (813) 695-4573
Dave Prickett, Chokoloskee, (813) 695-2286
Glenn Puopolo, Bonita Springs, (813) 353-4807
Kenny Shannon, Venice, (813) 497-4876
Russ Sirmons, St. Petersburg, (813) 526-2090
Tom Tamanini, (813)581-4942
Johnny Walker, Sarasota, (813) 922-2287
Mark Ward, Naples, (813) 775-9849
James Wood, Terra Ceia, (813) 722-8746

CHAPTER 18

SOUTH OF THE BORDER SNOOKING

THOUGH A CENTRAL AMERICA snook trip may seem too expensive and exotic for a lot of backcountry plug tossers, the costs and the problems of international travel are less than you might imagine. In fact, you can visit some of the prime trophy waters of Costa Rica for just a bit more than you'd pay, per day, for a guided trip here in the states, and down there, the price includes food and accommodations. You can spend a week at the edge of the Caribbean, including boats, guides, accommodations, sumptuous food and drink, and air transport, for $1,200 to $1,500 at this writing. Considering that guide fees alone in the states would equal that amount for a week of fishing, you can see that it's not a bad deal, and a visit here gives you a shot at more world-class fish than you're likely to see anywhere else in years.

All of the snook camps are located at river mouths on the northeast coast of Costa Rica. To get there, you fly commercial jets from Miami or Tampa to San Jose, the capitol city in the central part of the country. Most packages include an overnight in San Jose in a luxury hotel that's a match for anything in the states. You'll find the city far above the standards found in the rest of Central America, and the populace likes Americans just fine. San Jose is located in the mountains, and it's usually cool, though humid.

Shortly after dawn on your second day, you board a six-passenger plane to fly out to your camp. It's about a 40-minute jaunt, over spectacular mountain scenery that fades into coastal jungle, an

149

enormous carpet of green barely scratched by roads or habitations beyond small farming villages.

The camps are within a few minutes of the airstrips, and as soon as you stow your gear, you're ready to meet your guide and go fishing. The local villagers all make their living by fishing, and they keep tabs on the fish movement. They all also speak English, though some a lot better than others.

October is the prime month for giant snook in the surf and at the mouths of the Colorado, Parismina and Tortuguero rivers. During this time, snook of 30 pounds and up cruise the murky waves, looking for anything they can fit down their gallon-sized mouths. Three of the present line-class IGFA world records, including the 53-pound, 10-ounce all-tackle record, were taken in October in Costa Rica. The last two weeks of September can also be very good for trophy fish.

For perhaps smaller fish, but more of them, the last weeks of January are good, as are all the spring months if the rain and wind allow the surf to calm a bit. The spring fish are usually found from just inside the inlet to well up the rivers. They rarely weigh more than 10 pounds, but you can expect to catch 20 per rod or better when they're hitting, and some guys have had hundred-fish days here in recent seasons. You'll catch about as many "fat snook" as common snook fishing the inside, but they're just as feisty as their bigger brothers on the hook.

Fishing the surf generally requires wading, and it takes a bit of getting used to if you're new to the idea of sloshing out into three-foot rollers in an area noted for its shark population. No wade fisherman has yet had a serious shark problem, however it's not uncommon to lose a fish to the local version of Jaws.

Half-ounce black bucktails trimmed with a strip of pork rind are among the local favorites for fishing the surf in fall for the lunkers. These are slow-hopped along the bottom on two-hand baitcasters loaded with 200 yards or more of 20-pound test. The best action is often at dawn or dusk.

Another technique, often used by local commercial fishermen who make their catches by hook and line only, is to throw a 52M MirrOlure into the inlet waters, then reel it back as fast as they can turn the reel handle. It's a tremendously tiring way to fish, but also

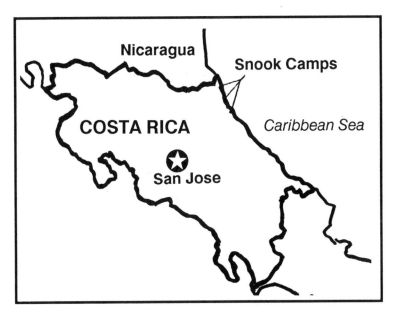

very effective. You'll also get some hook-ups by working the MirrOlure in the conventional slow-pump pattern. It's usually not fast fishing, but you can expect to connect with a giant or two daily-- and you're also very likely to tangle with a whopper tarpon.

(Speaking of silver kings, there's some of the world's best action for these giants just outside the inlets. Many anglers fish snook early and late, and spend the middle part of the day in a boat battling tarpon on the outside.) To catch the smaller snook on the inside, you fish much like you would in mangrove country back home, hitting points and eddies and casting topwaters, slow-sinkers and jigs up against the shoreline. Dark fly-rod streamers also work well at times.

You may also do some fast action on schooling fat snook by pitching an eighth-ounce plastic shad-type jig to surfacing fish. They roll like baby tarpon at times, and a small jig settling in front of their noses usually draws a prompt take.

The camps are all very comfortable and civilized, with generator-supplied electricity, running water that does not seem to do bad things to North American stomachs, hot showers and ceiling fans. There's no air conditioning, but you won't need it. You may get very hot and sticky while you're out in the boat in the heat of the day, but when you return to camp at night, the cool air from the mountains to the west rolls down the valleys toward the sea, dropping temperatures to a pleasant level quickly.

Parismina Tarpon Rancho is the oldest camp in the area, and one of the best. The adjacent waters have produced three of the current world records, including the all-tackle 53-10 and the number three fish, 43-8. Parismina is within walking distance of the mouth of the Parismina River where the giant fish have been caught, which allows easy access early and late, the prime times.

Rio Parismina Lodge is a new resort facility offering first class accommodations, a swimming pool, jacuzzi, and most importantly, 21-foot modified V-hull boats that are well suited for accessing the Gulf and fishing around the mouth of the river.

Archie Fields' Rio Colorado Lodge is a delightful maze of raised boardwalks, quaint bedrooms and tiki bars, and Archie's own collection of Costa Rican animals, including a semi-tame ocelot (don't put your fingers in his cage, even when he purrs!) parrots and monkeys. Fields has designed the camp so that you can get to any section without ever stepping down into the mud, or getting out in the rain. There's even a big-screen tv with satellite dish, so you can watch U.S. football if you go in fall.

You need a passport to travel to Costa Rica, and the tourist card you will be given on the flight from the U.S. to San Jose. No special vaccinations are required for entry.

Include a rain suit in your gear. And if you want to provide your guide with a tip he'll really appreciate, take him a moderately priced rain suit as well. The locals often use plastic garbage bags to protect themselves from the frequent showers. Digital watches are also much-admired among the guides, as are American sneakers.

To book trips into Rio Colorado Lodge, call (800) 243-9777. The number at Casa Mar is (800) 327-2880. Book Isla De Pesca, Parismina and Tortuga Lodge through PanAngling, (312) 263-0328. To book a trip to the Rio Parismina Lodge, call (800) 338-5688.

There's also good snook fishing in the coastal rivers of Belize, particularly the Manatee and the Main. Snook and tarpon fishing is now being developed in the jungle rivers of northern Venezuela, as well. For details on the Belize fishing, contact PanAngling at (312) 263-0328. For details on Venezuela, contact Fishing International at (813) 935-3141.

Frank Sargeant's INSHORE LIBRARY

The Snook Book is the first in a series of saltwater fishing books dedicated to the inshore angler. The series, known as the Inshore Library, includes complete details on how to find and catch America's favorite coastal species, and includes expert tips from dozens of the nation's finest coastal anglers.

These Editions Will Be Available Soon!

THE TROUT BOOK
THE REDFISH BOOK
THE TARPON BOOK
and others...

Don't Miss Them!

If you want to receive our catalog and other information about the availability of additional books in Frank Sargeant's Inshore Library, please fill out the following and mail today!

Yes, keep me updated on the Inshore Library books.

Name_____

Address_____

City, State, Zip_____

Mail to:
Larsen's Outdoor Publishing, Dept. SB
2640 Elizabeth Place
Lakeland, FL 33813

LARSEN'S OUTDOOR PUBLISHING
CONVENIENT ORDER FORM

Please send me additional copies of this book.

THE SNOOK BOOK
A Complete Angler's Guide
by Frank Sargeant

Price is only $11.95 each, which includes postage and handling.

Discount 10% if ordering two or three books. Discount 20% if ordering four or more books. Please allow three weeks for delivery. Thanks.

NAME_____

ADDRESS_____

CITY_____STATE_____ZIP_____

Number of books being ordered = _____ x $11.95

TOTAL AMOUNT ENCLOSED
(Check or Money Order) $_____

Copy this page and mail to:
Larry Larsen
Larsen's Outdoor Publishing
Dept. "BK-SB"
2640 Elizabeth Place
Lakeland, FL 33813

FOR THE SNOOK FISHERMEN
WHO ALSO FISH FOR
FRESH WATER BASS!

LARRY LARSEN'S BASS SERIES LIBRARY!

I. FOLLOW THE FORAGE FOR BETTER BASS ANGLING - VOLUME 1 BASS/ PREY RELATIONSHIP - The most important key to catching bass is finding them in a feeding mood. Knowing the predominant forage, its activity and availability, as well as its location in a body of water will enable an angler to catch more and larger bass. Whether you fish artificial lures or live bait, you will benefit from this book.

SPECIAL FEATURES   o PREDATOR/FORAGE INTERACTION
                                o BASS FEEDING BEHAVIOR
                                o UNDERSTANDING BASS FORAGE
                                o BASS/PREY PREFERENCES
                                o FORAGE ACTIVITY CHART

II. FOLLOW THE FORAGE FOR BETTER BASS ANGLING - VOLUME 2 TECH-NIQUES - Beginners and veterans alike will achieve more success utilizing proven concepts that are based on predator/forage interactions. Understanding the reasons behind lure or bait success will result in highly productive, bass-catching patterns.

SPECIAL FEATURES   o LURE SELECTION CRITERIA
                                o EFFECTIVE PATTERN DEVELOPMENT
                                o NEW BASS CATCHING TACTICS
                                o FORAGING HABITAT
                                o BAIT AND LURE METHODS

III. BASS PRO STRATEGIES - Professional fishermen have opportunities to devote extended amounts of time to analyzing a body of water and planning a productive day on it. They know how changes in pH, water temperature, color and fluctuations affect bass fishing, and they know how to adapt to weather and topographical variations. This book reveals the methods that the country's most successful tournament anglers have employed to catch bass almost every time out. The reader's productivity should improve after spending a few hours with this compilation of techniques!

SPECIAL FEATURES
- o MAPPING & WATER ELIMINATION
- o LOCATE DEEP & SHALLOW BASS
- o BOAT POSITION FACTORS
- o WATER CHEMISTRY INFLUENCES
- o WEATHER EFFECTS
- o TOPOGRAPHICAL TECHNIQUES

IV. BASS LURES - TRICKS & TECHNIQUES - Modifications of lures and development of new baits and techniques continue to keep the fare fresh, and that's important. Bass seem to become "accustomed" to the same artificials and presentations seen over and over again. As a result, they become harder to catch. It's the new approach that again sparks the interest of some largemouth. To that end, this book explores some of the latest ideas for modifying, rigging and using them. The lure modifications, tricks and techniques presented within these covers will work anywhere in the country.

SPECIAL FEATURES
- o UNIQUE LURE MODIFICATIONS
- o IN-DEPTH VARIABLE REASONING
- o PRODUCTIVE PRESENTATIONS
- o EFFECTIVE NEW RIGGINGS
- o TECHNOLOGICAL ADVANCES

V. SHALLOW WATER BASS - Catching shallow water largemouth is not particularly difficult. Catching lots of them usually is. Even more challenging is catching lunker-size bass in seasons other than during the spring spawn. Anglers applying the information within the covers of this book on marshes, estuaries, reservoirs, lakes, creeks or small ponds should triple their results. The book details productive new tactics to apply to thin-water angling. Numerous photographs and figures easily define the optimal locations and proven methods to catch bass.

SPECIAL FEATURES
- o UNDERSTANDING BASS/COVER INTERFACE
- o METHODS TO LOCATE BASS CONCENTRATIONS
- o ANALYSIS OF WATER TYPES
- o TACTICS FOR SPECIFIC HABITATS
- o LARSEN'S "FLORA FACTOR"

VI. BASS FISHING FACTS - This angler's guide to the lifestyles and behavior of the black bass is a reference source of sorts, never before compiled. The book explores the behavior of bass during pre- and post-spawn as well as during bedding season. It examines how bass utilize their senses to feed and how they respond to environmental factors. The book details how fishermen can be more productive by applying such knowledge to their bass angling. The information within the covers of this book includes those bass species, known as "other" bass, such as redeye, Suwannee, spotted, etc.

SPECIAL FEATURES
- o BASS FORAGING MOTIVATORS
- o DETAILED SPRING MOVEMENTS
- o A LOOK AT BASS SENSES
- o GENETIC INTRODUCTION/STUDIES
- o MINOR BASS SPECIES & HABITATS

158

VII. TROPHY BASS - is focused at today's dedicated lunker hunters who find more enjoyment in wrestling with one or two monster largemouth than with a "panfull" of yearlings. To help the reader better understand how to catch big bass, a majority of this book explores productive techniques for trophies. The "how to" information was gleaned from professional guides and other experienced trophy bass hunters. This book takes a look at the geographical areas and waters that offer better opportunities to catch giant bass.

SPECIAL FEATURES
- o GEOGRAPHIC DISTRIBUTIONS
- o STATE RECORD INFORMATION
- o GENETIC GIANTS
- o TECHNIQUES FOR TROPHIES
- o LOCATION CONSIDERATIONS
- o LURE AND BAIT TIMING

VIII. AN ANGLER'S GUIDE TO BASS PATTERNS examines the most effective combination of lure, method and places. Being able to develop a pattern of successful methods and lures for specific habitats and environmental conditions is the key to catching several bass on each fishing trip. Understanding bass movements and activities and the most appropriate and effective techniques to employ will add many pounds of enjoyment to the sport of bass fishing. "Bass Patterns" is a reference source for all anglers, regardless of where they live or their skill level.

SPECIAL FEATURES
- o BOAT POSITIONING
- o NEW WATER STRATEGIES
- o DEPTH AND COVER CONCEPTS
- o MOVING WATER TACTICS
- o WEATHER/ACTIVITY FACTORS
- o TRANSITIONAL TECHNIQUES

LARSEN'S OUTDOOR PUBLISHING

CONVENIENT ORDER FORM
ALL PRICES INCLUDE POSTAGE/HANDLING

FRESH WATER

___BSL1. Better Bass Angling Vol 1 ($13.95)
___BSL2. Better Bass Angling Vol 2 ($13.95)
___BSL3. Bass Pro Strategies ($13.95)
___BSL4. Bass Lures/Techniques ($13.95)
___BSL5. Shallow Water Bass ($13.95)
___BSL6. Bass Fishing Facts ($13.95)
___BSL7. Trophy Bass ($13.95)
___BSL8. Bass Patterns ($13.95)
___BSL9. Bass Guide Tips ($13.95)
___CF1. Mstrs' Scrts/Crappie Fshng ($12.45)
___CF2. Crappie Tactics ($12.45)
___CF3. Mstr's Secrets of Catfishing ($12.45)
___LB1. Larsen on Bass Tactics ($15.95)
___PF1. Peacock Bass Explosions! ($16.95)
___PF2. Peacock Bass & Other Fierce
         Exotics ($17.95)

SALT WATER

___IL1. The Snook Book ($13.95)
___IL2. The Redfish Book ($13.95)
___IL3. The Tarpon Book ($13.95)
___IL4. The Trout Book ($13.95)
___SW1. The Reef Fishing Book ($16.45)

OTHER OUTDOORS BOOKS

___DL1. Diving to Adventure ($12.45)
___DL2. Manatees/Vanishing ($12.45)
___DL3. Sea Turtles/Watchers' ($12.45)
___OC1. Outdoor Chuckle Book ($9.95)

REGIONAL

___FG1. Secret Spots-Tampa Bay/
         Cedar Key ($15.95)
___FG2. Secret Spots - SW Florida ($15.95)
___BW1. Guide/North Fl. Waters ($14.95)
___BW2. Guide/Cntral Fl.Waters ($14.95)
___BW3. Guide/South Fl.Waters ($14.95)
___OT1. Fish/Dive - Caribbean ($11.95)
___OT3. Fish/Dive Florida/ Keys ($13.95)

HUNTING

___DH1. Mstrs' Secrets/ Deer Hunting ($13.95)
___DH2. Science of Deer Hunting ($13.95)
___DH3. Mstrs' Secrets/Bowhunting ($12.45)
___DH4. How to Take Monster Bucks ($13.95)
___TH1. Mstrs' Secrets/ Turkey Hunting ($13.95)
___OA1. Hunting Dangerous Game! ($9.95)
___OA2. Game Birds & Gun Dogs ($9.95)
___BP1. Blackpowder Hunting Secrets ($14.45)

VIDEO &
SPECIAL DISCOUNT PACKAGES

___ V1 - Video - Advanced Bass Tactics $29.95
___BSL -Bass Series Library (9 vol. set) $94.45
___ IL - Inshore Library (4 vol. set) $42.95
___BW - Guides to Bass Waters (3 vols.) $37.95

Volume sets are autographed by each author.

BIG MULTI-BOOK DISCOUNT!
2-3 books, SAVE 10%
4 or more books, SAVE20%

INTERNATIONAL ORDERS
Send check in U.S. funds; add $6
more per book for airmail rate

ALL PRICES INCLUDE POSTAGE/HANDLING

No. of books _____ *x $* ____ *ea =$* _____   *Special Package* _____ *@ $* _____
No. of books _____ *x $* ____ *ea =$* _____   *Video (50-min) $29.95 = $* _____
Multi-book Discount (___ *%) $* _____   *(Pkgs include discount)= N/A*
SUBTOTAL 1 ___ *$* _____   *SUBTOTAL 2* ___ *$* _____

_____ **For Priority Mail (add $2 more per book)** $ _____
TOTAL ENCLOSED (check or money order) $ _____

NAME _____ *ADDRESS* _____

CITY _____ *STATE* _____ *ZIP* _____

Send check or Money Order to: Larsen's Outdoor Publishing, Dept. 97-BK
2640 Elizabeth Place, Lakeland, FL 33813 (941)644-3381
(Sorry, no credit card orders)